I met Don when he joined the first of many coaching ... years ago. I was immediately impressed with his heart for pastors and his desire to do the hard work of building God's church with excellence. During our time together, I have watched Don apply key truths and principles of church growth that have helped him turn his own church around. Now, he is effectively leading others to do the same.

Nelson Searcy
Lead Pastor of The Journey Church
Founder of www.ChurchLeaderInsights.com

"Turnaround Pastor tells the unvarnished story of leading a church through a genuine turnaround. Rather than a quick fix or gimmick approach, Don Ross shares practical insights on how to navigate the inevitable rough waters of church turnaround. His candid assessment provides a template to help any turnaround pastor lead strategically."

Dr. J. Melvyn Ming
Executive Director of Pastoral Care & Development
Northwest Ministry Network

Turning around a struggling church is one of the toughest jobs a pastor faces. Yet, this is exactly what nearly 80% of pastors are asked to do. *Turnaround Pastor*, by Don Ross, is a helpful resource to show pastors why and how a church turnaround can happen. You'll identify with his story of turning around a church, while gaining valuable insight on how to lead a turnaround in your church.

Gary L. McIntosh,
Talbot School of Theology, Biola University, La Mirada, CA
Author of *Taking Your Church to the Next Level*

If you are in leading a church that needs revitalization and redirection, specifically a turnaround, don't make any moves before reading this book. Don Ross has all three essential qualities necessary for writing a book on turning around a church: experience, knowledge, and passion.

I have never hesitated to recommend Don Ross as a quality consultant on turning a church around. Now with this book I am pleased to recommend him as a quality author, as well!

Charles Arn
Visiting Professor of Outreach, Wesley Seminary (Indiana)
and author of *What Every Pastor Should Know*

"Wow... what a great book. Don Ross actually tells the truth! I'm impressed and amazed with his transparency. If you currently find yourself squinting for a light of hope at the end of your tunnel of despair read this book."

Jim Henderson
Author of *Jim and Casper Go to Church*

The leadership insights Don offers from his pastoral experience are valuable to any reader, and particularly valuable to the leader who has been called to nurture a hurting or dying church back to wholeness and health. Unhealthy churches are not able to engage with the Mission of God effectively, and require special care and attention that will lead them back to health.

Don offers just that sort of insight, and does so in practical and engaging ways. The principles he offers are Biblically sound. The practical suggestions are useful in almost any situation and within reach of the leader who will lean into the Holy Spirit and set their mind to the task. Unhealthy established churches deserve to become healthy, and must do so in order to fulfill their intended mission.

Don's experience and testing as a leader afford him a unique perspective and leadership voice in a critical arena. I personally know and love this author, which always enhances my interest in what is written. This is a book worth reading.

Les Welk
Northwest Ministry Network Superintendent

Most memoirs are about the past, but Don Ross tells his story in a way that can foretell the future of your church! Experience and wisdom come together in a way that will turn you around—the first move towards a turnaround church.

Joseph Castleberry,
President of Northwest University
and author of *The Kingdom Net: Learning to Network Like Jesus* (My Healthy Church, 2013).

Turnaround Pastor is a must read for any pastor leading a turnaround church. Don Ross in an honest and transparent style presents the enormous challenges of being a turnaround pastor. He then offers very real and practical advice on how to overcome these challenges. I predict that thousands of churches will benefit from this book.

Steve Reynolds Pastor,
Capital Baptist Church, Annandale, VA
Author, *Bod4God* and *Get Off The Couch*

"Two words came to mind when I read Turnaround Pastor: "real" and "wisdom." Real because the stories Don shares are filled with unflinching realism that every pastor can relate to. This is not a sanitized note written in an ivory tower. Don's advice matters because he's writing from the front lines of ministry. Wisdom because this book is filled with hard earned chunks of practical wisdom. No theories here. The "Turnaround Change Cycle" concept alone is worth the price of the book.

Steve Pike,
National Director, Church Multiplication Network
Springfield, MO

Turnaround Pastor speaks to the church leader who is called to lead lethargic, tired, cynical, and even antagonistic congregations to regain their sense of purpose. Through his experiences with pain and perseverance, Don Ross discusses—with transparency—critical issues and principles that will help leaders fulfill their trusted calling to revitalize dying churches. Don, has not only discovered ways to invigorate churches but he gives encouragement, hope, and relevant tools to leaders who have been trusted with the wonderful calling to bring health to a church.

Wayde Goodall, D.Min
Dean, College of Ministry Northwest University
and Author of *Why Great Men Fall* and *Success Kills*

What makes Don a great author and leader is his humanity comes alive in his writings. Don writes with compassion and clarity. His authenticity is breathtaking. He has been broken by Jesus and writes from heart of humility.
Don's book is refreshing in a day where so many mainline denominations are focusing on church planting, but Jesus also wants to wake up the established church. Don's story and practical insights will encourage and strengthen any pastor who dares says "yes" to Jesus in leading a Turnaround Church.

Troy Jones
Lead Pastor,
New Life Church, Renton

This is a book that every pastor should read. It is especially critical if you pastor a church that has plateaued or is in decline, but both the story Don tells of his own experience leading a turnaround church and the important principles he shares to facilitate a turnaround will be helpful to any pastor.

Although Don's examples are from churches and resources in North America, most of the things he shares are universal, and can and should speak to any pastor anywhere in the world today.

In the first half of the book Don inspires and challenges us with his own personal journey. In the second half he shares principles and strategies that can be brought into a turnaround situation. In fact, many of these principles can be a great help to every church at every stage of the churches history. Story and training combine to feed both the heart and the mind. Don's openness about his own experience and his comforting encouragement to pastors make this book a valuable tool for any pastor. I recommend this book highly.

Dave Kenney
Lead Pastor, International English Service
Jakarta, Indonesia

What made *Turnaround Pastor* so riveting for me is the reality that Don has coached me for almost 20 years, been my biggest cheerleader and a trusted confidant. We first met when I became his youth pastor in Lynden, WA where the church drama that he writes about in chapter 2 took place. That battle forged our friendship. In the ensuing years, and over hundreds of cups of coffee, I had a front row seat to his "turnaround church" journey.

When I read *Turnaround Pastor*, I had "insider knowledge" that not all readers will have. My hunch is that if you plan to read further, you too are living with a level of pain due to some kind of tension related to your current ministry realities. As a friend, colleague, and recipient of Don's coaching, I invite you to read on with just one thought: This is not theory, but wisdom with scars.

Scott Harris
Lead Pastor, Brooklake Church
Federal Way, WA

TURNAROUND PASTOR

TURNAROUND PASTOR

Pathways to Save, Revive
and Build Your Church

DONALD ROSS

Turnaround Church Coaching Network
7011 226th Place SW
Montlake Terrace, WA 98043

Printed in the United States of America

17 16 15 14 13   1 2 3 4

ISBN: 978-0-989769-8-08

Library of Congress Control Number: 2013946554

*This book is dedicated to my beautiful wife Brenda,
whose steadfast support during our church turnaround
inspired me to explore new pathways and break barriers
even at the toughest of times.*

CONTENTS

ACKNOWLEDGEMENT

This book is about Creekside Church and I love Creekside Church. I want to thank them for their continued love and support as we experimented, struggled, failed and finally succeeded in seeing our church began to live up to our kingdom potential. They believed even when they couldn't see, gave more when it seemed they'd given all, and trusted God to reach people they didn't know, and then perhaps they gave the greatest gift of all, they welcomed everyone who came.

INTRODUCTION

I LOVE PASTORS.

I love being a pastor, teaching pastors, hanging out with pastors, and encouraging pastors. That's why I wrote this book.

Eric Reed, of *Leadership Journal*, writes that 19,200 pastors annually are required to leave the ministry (*Leadership Journal*, January, 2006). Most leave the ministry due to tension and stress, but money, depression, leadership confusion, and lack of a clear strategy for moving their church forward also play a role.

In addition, the resistance encountered in leading an established church into a better day, or even to moderate survival, is unimaginable by most people's standards. My hope and heartfelt prayer is that this book will help stem the tide on that decrease of Godly leaders, at least to some degree.

By God's grace, and I mean that genuinely, I was called to lead a declining church back into health and growth. I faced just about every kind of problem you can imagine as a part of my assignment, and Jesus is asking me to share with you what I've learned.

It is your choice to accept or reject what you read in the chapters ahead of you, but I have done my best to give you all the information I can so that you can make wise decisions.

Turnaround Pastor is a book for pastors, written in two parts. The first part is a story of pain and redemption, growth and learning, both public and private. I have been called to let you peek behind the curtain and walk vicariously with me on a journey lived out over two decades. Leading a turnaround church is not a quick chore—let's be clear about that. As you will read in the first chapter, Jesus gave His life for us, and He has no problem asking us to give a decade or two for one local church. That being said, I believe that if I had

had a book similar to this one, it could have cut our turnaround time dramatically.

The second part of this book is about developing a course of action for your church. It includes both strategy and tactics for leading a turnaround church. You will receive ideas, facts, ratios, and resources to help you do what God has called you to do.

I wrestled greatly with this format: a book in two parts. I considered blending the teaching in with the story, and I did do that somewhat. But for the most part, the application, the "how-to," will come in the second half.

My hope is that you will read both and not simply skip to the second half to cherry-pick the ideas. If you do, my guess is that you'll be back reading the first part of the book sometime in the future, and here's why: The first half of the book is about the spiritual and emotional price tag associated with leading a turnaround church. With all my heart, I have to say that leading a turnaround church is more about *being* than *doing*. Who you are is infinitely more important than what you know or what you can do.

Jesus spent much more time preparing me to lead than He ever did teaching me to lead. In America, we love to focus on how to do something, but Jesus wants to focus on who we are. And there is a great truth here, in understanding why Jesus has this priority of heart over skill, because our skill connects us to the task, but our heart connects us to God.

When God created the earth, He made it so that everything that was created would reproduce after its own kind. He did this for plants, animals, and leaders. As leaders, we reproduce leaders in a similar vein as ourselves, so it makes sense that Jesus would focus on the heart.

When Jesus developed leaders, He often said, "Follow this example," as in communion, or, "Teach and baptize like this," as in the Great Commission. If Jesus reproduced leaders after His "own kind," don't you think we will too? And the leaders we reproduce will either be focused on heart issues or a leadership skill set. The heart must come first, then the training and skill development; and I have followed that model in this book.

My prayer for you as you read this material is that you'll be inspired and equipped, encouraged and informed, and that you choose to live up to the potential Jesus has instilled in you. When you know you are putting a smile on Jesus' face, though you may be in a desperate situation personally, you know the sacrifice is worth it.

◄ 1 ►

DANCING BLINDFOLDED
IN A MINEFIELD

GROWING UP, I LOVED WATCHING WAR MOVIES with my dad. I still do, and I now feel the tension shown in war movies often represents what we feel in church leadership. We face dangerous situations, any one of which could wound us or completely remove us from the ministry.

In the war classic *Anzio*, there is a scene where an entire company of US Rangers is ambushed. Many are killed, and others are taken prisoner. But one platoon escapes and finds refuge in an abandoned farmhouse.

They are safe until a German tank discovers them and lines up to destroy the house. So they escape out the back, only to face a minefield blocking their path. They are stymied until a news correspondent, played by Robert Mitchum, who is attached to the platoon, comes up with an idea to help them escape.

They decide to throw large stones into the minefield to create a safe path across. If a stone lands on a mine, it explodes, and no one is hurt. If the thrown stone lands without hitting a mine, they can step on it and proceed safely across the field.

The soldiers use this plan, and it works fine for a while. But the tension increases as the German tank gets closer and closer. When most of the platoon is across the minefield, and just as the tank is crashing through the house, one last soldier makes a dash across the stone path.

As this last soldier is partially across the stones, he starts to lose his balance. He finds himself tipping toward the unsafe earth, inches away from an area that could contain a mine. In the background you can hear the tank crashing closer and closer. Finally, the soldier regains his balance and rushes to safety with the rest of the platoon.

I bought this movie on DVD, and I found myself watching this scene again and again. As this last soldier crossed the minefield, I heard the noise of the tank crashing through the house, I heard his friends cheering him on, and I saw him balancing on a stone in the middle of a minefield. It looked like he was dancing. Then he finally regained his balance and escaped.

I remember thinking the only thing that would have made this situation worse was if this soldier had to cross the minefield blindfolded. Imagine having the enemy pursuing you, danger inches away with your very future at stake, and you can't see with clarity where you are going.

It was then I realized my assignment at my church was exactly like this soldier's predicament. I was blindfolded. I was the soldier balancing on a stone in a minefield in this story—scared, under pressure, with the feeling of being trapped in a situation I really didn't sign up for, with very little clarity about my future.

Turnaround Pastor is the story of a local church's movement from mere survival toward health, from having no mission to embracing a clear mission, and from despair to genuine hope. It is a simple story of purpose, as Christ restores and heals His broken church. It is also a very complicated story of pain, patience, process, and balance.

Imagine if crossing the minefield didn't take minutes, but years—fifteen years in our case. In that situation, surviving the tension of the process becomes as important as surviving the minefield. Either one can kill you.

Then add the blindfold, which is the reality of leading a turnaround process in a declining church with a long history. The blindfold keeps you from seeing clearly and being decisive as a leader. Almost every decision becomes a guess because of incomplete and inconclusive information.

A new leader of a turnaround church is blind to his church's history. He didn't live it, and the other leaders can only retell the history of their church as they experienced it, which may or may not be helpful. It is entirely possible that the leader could slip off the rock and step on a mine by saying something that touches this church's history in a bad way. That will slow down progress and could even lead to his removal.

A new leader is also blind to the finances of his church. I don't really care how clear the budget or accounting system is; he is still blind. He doesn't know how the money was raised or misused in the past. He doesn't know what key phrases illicit strong feelings or what buzzwords are loaded. It is very easy to slip off the rock and step on a money mine.

Often a new turnaround leader will inherit existing staff. The congregation's loyalty to existing staff is much higher than to a new pastor. The fact that you are in the key position of leadership is virtually meaningless until you have established yourself. Many in your church are actually waiting to see if you will make it. They wonder, "Will this leader survive?"

Facilities and buildings are another minefield. Every established church has skeletons in their buildings (figuratively, not literally, I hope). For example, you may think that simply painting the nursery would bring kudos to a new pastor. What you didn't know was, the last nursery paint color was picked out by a loving, elderly woman who recently died. No one is painting the room as a memorial to her, but if you repaint the room, unknown to you, her memory will be insulted. *Boom!* You just blew up a land mine.

The board or lay leadership is probably the most dangerous part of the minefield. As a new leader you have no idea what the culture is in the boardroom. Are you the leader, setting the agenda, or is this the meeting where you come to receive your assignments for the next month from the real leaders? If you miss this signal, you'll be badly and repeatedly wounded from an ecclesiastical, anti-personnel mine.

Do I need to go any further in painting the picture of this minefield? Leading an established church in a turnaround process is very much like dancing blindfolded in a minefield, and you were called to do it by the one who raises the dead, the Lord Jesus Christ Himself.

In many ways, the challenge of a turnaround church was written for us 2,000 years ago in Revelation 3:1–3. The letter to the church of Sardis says,

To the angel of the church in Sardis write:
These are the words of him who holds the seven spirits of God
and the seven stars. I know your deeds; you have a <u>reputation</u>
<u>of being alive, but you are dead</u>. Wake up! <u>Strengthen what</u>
<u>remains and is about to die</u>, for I have not found your deeds
complete in the sight of my God. Remember, therefore, what
you have received and heard; obey it, and repent. But if you
do not wake up, I will come like a thief, and you will not know
at what time I will come to you.

In a sense, a declining church may have had a reputation of being alive, but it is not alive now. I know our church had the reputation of being alive. I'm told our church was the largest church in Seattle in the late 1980s, running 2,000 in Sunday morning attendance.

In the early years, when someone in our church reminded me of our past history and how large we had been, I would have to remind him or her I hadn't been there then and our church was no longer that way. I didn't win points with that response, by the way. It was my way of reminding our church that we had a "reputation of being alive, but we were dead" in mission.

It was a painful reminder, but it was necessary or the church would never discover our current reality. Without that discovery, we would have no future.

When you are called by Jesus to lead a turnaround church, you are called to "strengthen what remains and is about to die." To our knowledge, every one of the seven churches in Revelation went out of business, just like the more than 4,000 churches that go out of business each year in America.

Turnaround pastors are called to see a better day for the church they are leading. They must also be willing to endure the pain necessary to get the church there. The critical decisions to move a dying church forward toward health and mission are often painful and hard for those around them to see. In fact, just getting a church to admit it's dying may be the hardest thing of all.

In the movie *Men of Honor*, Cuba Gooding Jr. plays Carl Brashear, who was the first African-American to become a US Navy Master

Diver. He served from 1948–1979 and rose to the rank of Master Chief Petty Officer. Brashear runs up against the racist Master Chief Petty Officer Billy Sunday, played by Robert DeNiro. Sunday's duties include overseeing the navy's Diving and Salvage School, Bayonne, New Jersey, into which Brashear is inducted only through sheer determination.

At one point in the movie, Sunday is introducing the role of a navy diver to a class of trainees. He goes into great detail about the dangers, intensive training, physical hardship, and fear associated with such military operations. He then concludes with these words: "You stand a very good chance of dying cold and alone, 200 feet below the surface. I don't know why anyone would want to be a navy diver." But sailors were lined up to serve in spite of the danger.

If you are currently leading a turnaround church, you know that feeling of being cold and alone. You are one of God's navy divers, sent to salvage something that will be completely lost if you don't say, "Yes, I'll do this, Jesus." The environment is hard, the project is difficult, long, and labor-intensive.

You will probably minister in obscurity, at least for a while, like a navy diver. But Jesus will use you to give new life to something that is dying. If Jesus died to give birth to the church, would you be willing to give a decade or two of your life to save one?

If you are reading this book, you have probably already answered that question, and the answer is probably yes. My prayer for you, for this book, and for all who read it is that Jesus will use it to encourage faithful, dedicated leaders to "strengthen what remains."

America needs more churches. Our world needs more churches. We are all familiar with the church planting focus—and it is a wonderful focus—but we also need more turnaround churches.

Jesus' vision for reaching the world is bigger than just new churches. He loves resurrecting dead things as well. Take note that every time Jesus raised someone from the dead, someone who was already alive had faith to see the miracle happen.

Has Christ called you to lead a turnaround church? Are you willing to do "divine salvage work"? If you're interested in quick ministry results, this may not be your calling. If it's tough for you to work with potentially antagonistic alliances, maybe you should look elsewhere.

But if Christ has built a vision in you of a particular local church that may be more dead than alive, you're a candidate to lead a turnaround church. If you've dreamed of your declining church reversing trends and growing, you're a candidate to lead a turnaround church.

If you know Jesus has placed you in a dying situation and you're looking for answers to practical questions, you're a candidate to lead a turnaround church. And like a navy diver, you are my brother in a dangerous and exciting calling.

◄ 2 ►
INTRODUCTION TO CHURCH MINEFIELDS

WHEN A SOLDIER JOINS THE ARMY, his first day is induction day. He has committed to joining the army, but he only has a vague idea of what is ahead of him. Nevertheless, he is committed. He gets his head shaved and gets yelled at a lot. He receives new clothes and in general has his entire world turned upside down. But it is all for a greater purpose. That greater purpose is the security of a nation, and his personal discomfort is of little concern in light of a greater cause.

So it is with Jesus, who also has no problem turning our world upside down and causing us discomfort if it aids the greater cause of expanding His kingdom. This is not to say that Jesus arbitrarily causes us pain. That is certainly not the case. Jesus realizes, as He hopes we do also, that eternity for a lost person is much more painful than our temporary discomfort.

A defining moment in my leading of a turnaround church happened in August of 2004. Up to this point I was happy to simply be a local church pastor who was trying to help his church survive and hopefully grow. I had lowered all my personal expectations to simply making it through another week. Not very inspiring, is it?

It was a nice August day in Seattle, which means it wasn't raining. (If you've ever been to our city, you know we basically have two seasons: warm and rainy, and cold and rainy. We do have occasional sunny days, and they are rare and precious. This happened to be one of them.) As I reached into my mailbox at the office of The Northgate Church, my world was about to change. I had no idea that a simple postcard about another church selling their campus could rock my world, but it did.

I went through the mail, hoping for some good news, but really I was just wishing I weren't there. Honestly, I felt like leading this church was one big waste of time. I wanted to leave badly. After nine years of solid effort, I had very little to show, and in fact I felt like I'd lost ground. Jesus knew full well how I felt. I'd told him often. I loved these people but hated the situation.

This was my third church as a career pastor. The other two churches had grown well, but not this one. Was this just a tougher situation, or was I not "leader" enough to move it forward?

My first effort in 1983 as a young 27-year-old pastor saw a growth spike from 50 to 200 people in two years in a rural town of about 300 people. We built a new building. My family and I loved the congregation, and they loved us. I moved on after six successful years. I thought my whole career would be like this. I was so naive.

I took my second church in 1989, and it also grew well. Before I arrived, it had dropped from 600 to 350 due to internal turmoil and a pastoral change. I saw it grow from 350 to 800 in four years. Again we built a new addition by paying cash for it and upgrading our four-year-old campus to 35,000 square feet. I felt like I was on a roll.

I loved leading the congregation, and they seemed to love being led. We added ministries, new worship services, and staff; we were rapidly paying down the mortgage; people were coming to faith in Christ; and all seemed right with the world.

There was a growing feeling inside me, though, that something was fundamentally not right at this church. I didn't know it at the time, but Jesus was about to give me a crash course in minefield dancing. By *crash course*, I don't mean *quick*, I mean *crash*, as in, "I hit the wall going full speed" crash.

This church did not have a clear mission, except to perpetuate its past into the future. There were indicators that I did not have the board's full support and that conflict was just around the corner. I was young, 33, at the time and wasn't sure what to do, so I just kept going, hoping whatever was in my gut would go away. It didn't.

We continued to grow in both "nickels and noses" and began to receive recognition from denominational leaders. This recognition just spurred me to work harder and longer, which seemed to produce more positive results. Yet that nagging in my gut was growing also.

I was unaware of most of the negative signals, and I ignored the others I did see. So when a key leader verbally attacked me during a board meeting, and then again at a very well-attended church business meeting, I didn't know what to do. I was paralyzed emotionally. Nothing in my education or experience had prepared me for this situation.

People in the church sensed there was trouble, and hundreds had showed up to the business meeting to see what was going on. I just felt ambushed and outnumbered. My wife and I were traumatized.

I was shocked because this man had been such a good friend, or at least had seemed like it. He'd been instrumental in my coming to lead this church. Our family had stayed at their home, and theirs at ours. I was having trouble wrapping my head around the concept that such a good friend would oppose me like this. I've since learned that future antagonists often come disguised as good friends, but at the time I didn't have a clue. I was about to experience a series of huge ecclesiastical land mines exploding under my feet.

Now I faced a dilemma. In order for me to defend myself, I would have to attack other church leaders and give impetus to a church fight. I didn't want to do that. If you've ever been in a church fight, you know how devastating it is to the people, how dishonoring it is to Jesus, and how it usually accomplishes nothing. In addition, church turmoil raises the tension in a church's culture, and sheep do not do well with tension. In fact, they run from it. This new leadership threat was focused not only at me but at all I had helped build. This emerging church fight threatened the spiritual walk of new believers and the growth we'd experienced.

If I didn't defend myself, however, I would no longer be the pastor. I'd be out of a job with no way to support my family or lead those who had come to Christ. I didn't want that to happen either. My stomach was in knots. I didn't realize I had come face-to-face with a real-life antagonist who was triggering land mines directly in my path. I'll speak more on that later.

I went home with this feeling of impending doom hanging over my head. Within a few days I received a phone call; the board wanted to meet with me. I had a pretty good idea about what was coming, and it wasn't going to be pleasant. But like a man facing the gallows, I decided to "man up" and walk through this season of crisis.

I wasn't being brave; I just had no other choice. I remember thinking about a spider I'd seen trapped in a sink, spiraling down the drain, helpless to do anything about it. The spider scrambled to get out of the force of the water but to no avail. That was exactly how I felt.

I remember praying and telling Jesus this wasn't fair, and that I wanted Him to rescue me. He said nothing. Then I told Him that I'd been faithful to Him, that we'd seen good fruit, and that I deserved to be rescued from this situation. Again, He said nothing.

Finally, after exhausting in prayer every argument I could think of to get Him to help me out of this predicament, I asked Jesus, "So how would you like me to play this out? What do you want me to do here?"

His answer came inside me, quick and clear. It was very memorable. He said, "Abandon yourself to My care." That was it. Nothing more. No instructions, no hopeful encouragement, just "Abandon yourself to My care." I felt like the spider again.

I walked through the door of our church conference room, to the follow-up board meeting after that terrible, public, and painful all-church business meeting. All seven deacons were at the table, along with a few others who were invited by them to join us. I remember again feeling very outnumbered.

I had brought my local denominational area leader for support. I was glad he was with me, but we were both powerless to bring any change to these events—and everyone in the room knew it. I was especially aware that this was serious and I was helpless. I prayed inside for wisdom. Nothing came, just some familiar words—"Trust Me"—and then the meeting started.

The Vice Chairman opened the meeting and got right to the point. He said, "Pastor Don, we've called you here because, in light of all that has gone on, perhaps it would be best if you would consider resigning. Would you consider resigning?"

When those words came out of his mouth, all heads in the room turned toward me. There was a moment of silence, and everyone waited to hear how I would respond. I felt like throwing up.

I had only one response, and now was the time to say it. So I sucked it up and said, "If you men no longer support me as your pastor, and leaving is all I have left, then I want to leave well."

I lied. Those words sounded good, but I really didn't want to leave well. I didn't want to leave at all. I knew the congregation was with me and I could fight this. I wanted to defend myself and fight the board; that's what I really wanted to do. I wanted to scream and hit somebody, but I behaved and played my part. I did choose to "abandon myself to Jesus' care," but more than ever, I felt like that spider going down the drain.

With those few words, I was, for all intents and purposes, gone, fired. Technically I wasn't fired, it was an orchestrated resignation, but it still felt like I was being fired. I was being asked to resign at the board's request. That's an invitation you really can't say no to without further hurting the church or yourself.

We talked for a bit more, setting a date for the final service, salary payout, minimal severance, and some other details. But the real work of this meeting was over, and I only heard part of the conversation after it. I was emotionally numb and found it very hard to focus. I just wanted out. I wanted this scene to be over with.

There is no way to candy-coat this experience. I was fired. It was painful and public, and it seemed like everyone in our small town of 5,000 people knew about it within 24 hours. Humiliation was added to defeat as unsubstantiated rumors flew. Welcome to the ministry.

German theologian and pastor Dietrich Bonhoeffer said, "When Christ calls a man, he bids him come and die." I was personally learning some of the truth of that statement.

Although my leaving was painful due to intense conflict between the board and me, the church had grown during my four years there and was solid when I left. It did not stay that way, and that genuinely grieved me. The next pastor lasted 18 months. We became good friends and remain so to this day. Misery loves company, doesn't it?

I had learned a lot from leading my second church, and although this church had a history of rolling pastors down the road like used tires off a semi, I had to own my part in all that happened there.

I remember one of my classmates in seminary making a statement about pastors being fired. He said, "At some point in our career, we will all probably be fired. It is the nature of the leadership role Christ has called us to. We are change agents. All change agents induce pain, and people usually don't respond well to pain. So at some point they will take it out on us."

I remember thinking to myself when I heard that statement, "Any pastor who gets fired must be an idiot, sinful, or a very poor leader. I'm never going to get fired." I was pretty prideful and considered myself immune to such circumstances.

The good thing is that I didn't say that statement out loud. The bad thing is, I thought it. I was not an idiot or walking in sin, and I was a good leader, but I had been fired. I was the victim of circumstances I'd permitted, both in our church and in my life.

As I look back, there were three things that converged in my life, like the perfect storm, to bring about this event.

First of all, as I said, this church had a history of pushing pastors out. As a pastor's influence grew, and the congregation trusted him, the other leaders appeared threatened by that. I had talked with five of the previous pastors, and each one basically told me the same thing. At some point in their leadership of this church, they hit a leadership wall and were expelled.

Most of them were wise enough not to let themselves get fired. They saw the handwriting on the wall and left of their own volition, moving on to another church.

While I was the pastor, I had read through this church's history and their annual meetings, and it was amazing. The church battles raged over the most insignificant things, including an ongoing fight for eleven years about changing the time of the evening service by thirty minutes. It was routine for board meetings to last four or five hours, and annual business meetings often went from 7 PM to nearly 11 PM. The life-changing special business meeting I'd experienced went until well after midnight.

So as my influence grew in this church, I became more and more of a threat to the established leaders. I had no idea this was happening, which in turn actually threatened my leadership as well. The history of this church and how it had handled leadership issues and church conflict long before I arrived was a key factor. I should have researched that before coming, because it was a critical element in my being asked to leave.

The second major factor in my termination was the presence of an antagonist who was both my friend and on the church board. I had never dealt with an antagonist like this before.

Antagonist are people who create tension for the purpose of gaining power. They are self-serving, power-hungry, and more concerned about position than people. They are a sincere danger to any church, and like a wolf disguised as a sheep to attack a flock, they must be driven away for the safety of the flock.

This is not to say that everyone who disagrees with us pastors is an antagonist. That is certainly not the case, and we need to listen well to those who do disagree with us. There is safety and security when opposing views are presented, but everyone needs to be seeking the good of the church. Antagonists don't seek the good of the church. They seek their own agenda, whether it is good or not, and they are relentless.

There are three levels of church antagonists—minor, moderate, and major—with the most destructive being a major antagonist. Major antagonists don't just disagree, or even just raise tension. They want to take you out, and the worst ones don't care what it costs them in the process. That is exactly what I was up against, and I had no idea how to proceed, let alone the scope of my problem.

I have since learned that the uncomfortable and distasteful decision to confront them is the only way forward. As Kenneth Haugk says so eloquently in his book *Antagonists in the Church*, there is only one way to deal with a major antagonist. You must "drive them from the flock." I had had that opportunity earlier, and I had refused to take it. I paid the price for not being the loving leader I should have been. Unfortunately, the church also paid for my poor leadership. I am still genuinely sorry for that to this day.

I could have stopped him. I had begun to see this person as an antagonist when his name came up for a position on the board. I had facts that clearly disqualified him for service at the leadership level, but I refused to mention these facts out of fear.

I feared if I mentioned this man was unqualified, that I would have been asked how I came to know these facts and that my own leadership would have been placed under suspicion. I chose rather to remain silent and to try to control his behavior through our relationship. My decision was both dishonest and unsuccessful.

Our churches deserve good leaders. If I had been honest and shared why this man was unqualified, there would have been a disruption and maybe even a fight, but it would not have been a devastating series of explosions in our church minefield.

As leaders, we are always seeking a peaceful and tranquil environment for our church, but sometimes we have to choose between several small, personal, and painful explosions or the large, catastrophic ones. If we remain silent when we should speak up, and simply hope for the best, we risk more than we imagine. As my friend and coach, Nelson Searcy, says, "Hope is not a church strategy."

I am totally convinced to this day that if I would have spoken up and told the truth at that moment, instead of covering for this man, I would have remained as the pastor. I chose poorly, but I learned. In the last twenty years of ministry, I have had several opportunities to speak the uncomfortable truth or remain silent. Each time, I have chosen to speak up. I hated doing it, but not speaking up would have been far worse, for both the church and for me.

I was the third factor in this recipe of ecclesiastical pain. I'd pushed the church hard. I was proud and arrogant about what we'd accomplished. I'd bragged about our growth and my leadership, and at points my family paid the price too. After I'd resigned, I remember my wife telling me she liked me better when I wasn't a pastor. She felt she was always second to the church.

One night when we were out to dinner, she said, "I always felt like the church was your mistress. When you were with me, you always seemed to be thinking about *her*." That painful truth was difficult to hear. It was time for me to face up to some serious issues in my life. As a result, I sat out of pastoral ministry for the next two years.

I had to recognize that I could do nothing about this church's history any longer. I was out, and that was that. And furthermore, I could no longer do anything about the antagonist I'd faced. I'd learned a valuable lesson, but now the lesson was over. I could only work on the remaining third of the equation: myself. So I found myself again abandoned to the care of Jesus.

I knew I needed help to reorder my inner world. Emotionally, I was a mess. I dropped 30 pounds in eight weeks, had trouble sleeping, and was close to an emotional breakdown. I needed help to find out where in this story I was the victim and where I'd sabotaged my own success.

I couldn't answer these questions myself, so I joined a recovery group and also sought professional counseling to try and get a grip on what I'd been through in the last four years.

It was a good thing for me to sit out from being a pastor. I needed to rest and reflect on what I would do differently next time—if God were to trust me with a next time. Neither my wife nor I were anxious to get back into pastoral work after this experience. Recovery was slow.

During the two years I was not a pastor, I traveled as a church consultant, which I had done on a part-time basis for the previous ten years. I knew and understood churches and decided to put my skills to use in earning a living, but it was also very ironic. Here I was, a church consultant helping other churches get it right, and I had been asked to leave my own church. What an incredible sense of divine humor our God has.

Interestingly enough, God did use me to help others. Somehow it seems that genuine failure, coupled with painful insight and a dash of forced humility, qualifies you to help others (II Cor. 1:3–5). I really had very little trouble getting contracts with churches, and I look back on that time as both restful and filled with purpose.

I enjoyed my time traveling, but at the two-year mark I could feel a change coming. One day, as I was leading a lunch-hour workshop that focused on developing leadership influence in an aging congregation, one of the pastors came up to me and asked if I'd lead this same workshop for his board. I never said no to new business.

His name was Richard Vicknair, and he was the senior leader of North Seattle Christian Fellowship, the former name of The Northgate Church. I knew the church. I'd attended there as a student while doing my undergraduate work at Northwest University. I remembered it being very alive and having a powerful impact in Seattle.

Richard explained that the church had once been a beacon in Seattle, and now it was only a shadow of its former self. It had dropped from a high attendance of 2000 to around 350. The church was in pain due to its decline, and he was intrigued with what I'd presented that day.

Richard had been asked to be the interim pastor after some very painful years. The previous pastor of 30 years had left a mix of both productive ministry and intense congregational pain. Richard had served as interim for the last four years, and now the search was on again for a new senior leader. In my heart, I felt like I was being moderately scrutinized during this conversation, but I also felt a peace from God.

I met with the board and did my presentation. I remember during the meeting being filled with vision for this church—wondering, *What I would do if I were leading here?*—but I did my best to push these feelings down.

Was I ready to engage in being a pastor again? What about my wife and family? Could I deal with the inevitable tensions that would certainly come? Maybe the spider was starting to dry out.

INSIGHT FROM LEADERS

The first time I showed up at church was six months after Don Ross was hired. I was in a unique position. I had no history with the church. I wasn't part of a warring faction. I wasn't impressed by people who'd sat in the same sanctuary seats for a decade or longer. I wasn't even interested in joining a church. I came to give my young children a little exposure to religion. It had been twenty years since I'd stepped inside any house of worship except to attend a wedding or a funeral. I had no idea what to expect.

The campus was a hodgepodge of unimpressive buildings that looked like they'd been thrown together with less planning than a mining camp in the Old West. The church doors were solid and imposing as if designed to protect a fortress.

Though my three kids and I were greeted politely, the greeters seemed shocked to see us there. When Don got up to speak he talked about the variety of people living in the area who were unchurched and needed to feel welcomed here.

As far as welcome, I felt like I'd stumbled into a private club and didn't know the secret handshake. After the service I had coffee and mingled with the congregation. Some of them referred to Don as the new pastor in a tone that clearly showed their lack of enthusiasm.

I wasn't impressed. I stereotyped the congregants as people who hated sin and the sinner. I didn't want any part of a church full of self-declared saints. I kept coming back because of Don's passion and ability to make the Bible relevant to the modern world. He seemed different than the church environment. Within a few months I became a believer. I was the first new believer since Don began leading the church. Now baptismal services are frequent, large and enthusiastically attended.

Don became my friend as well as my pastor. I witnessed from the beginning the heartbreak and suffering he and the church experienced. Through it all he stayed the course that led to a changed heart and a changed church. The fortress mentality has become a mission mentality that literally reaches out to the community and the world.

Creekside Church hasn't just grown dramatically in numbers. More important is the growth of the spiritual depth of the congregation. I can only imagine how much faster Don could have turned the church around if he'd had a book like Turnaround Pastor to help him every step of the way.

Get your highlighters out and be prepared to enjoy a compelling and practical story of failure to success and pain to redemption. It's a riveting and inspiring read.

Robert D. Doell
Creekside Church Member
Author of *After Dinner Games*

◀ 3 ▶

EXPOSING THE MINEFIELDS

I'D LIKE TO TELL YOU THAT THE MOVE to my church in Seattle was smooth and easy, but it wasn't. It turns out, as many of you know, God puts us through challenging situations to prepare us for even more difficult circumstances.

A month after my presentation to the board, we were called and asked if we'd be willing to consider being the senior leaders at North Seattle Christian Fellowship. I said no. My wife was relieved.

Then they asked if we would pray about it. What could I say to that holy request? "No, I don't want to lead your church, and I don't want to talk to God about it either!"

I simply said, "Sure, I'll pray about it." In my heart, I knew I was surrendering to the next chapter of my life. The spider was back in the water again.

It was at this point my wife, Brenda, and I had a serious talk. I said I felt like there was something to this offer that we should pursue. She was unconvinced. She would have been totally satisfied if I continued doing church consulting work and never was a pastor again. The painful season we'd endured had marked both of us. I didn't push it.

About a week later I brought it up again, saying, "I still feel called to be a pastor. I've trained all my life to do this. I'm 75 percent through graduate school, working on a third degree. I think we need to look deeper into this opportunity in Seattle."

Then she surprised me, as she has done many times before, with stunning insight, both soft and quiet yet with an ability to shake my foundation. She said she would be willing to investigate further, but she had a personal request that had to be a part of the deal if we went further down this road.

She said, "Maybe God is leading us to move to Seattle, and if that is the case, I want to be obedient. I just don't want you whimsically moving us to Seattle. I want a veto vote on this move if I feel it will be another unsafe environment."

I was stunned and tried to mask my emotions, but I doubt that I did very well. I tried to maintain eye contact and respond without reacting. I delicately replied, "So what you are saying is, if I think we should move to Seattle, and you don't think we should, I need to let you quash that decision?"

She smiled lovingly and gently replied, "Yes, that's it exactly. If we agree that I have a veto vote to use if I feel this is another unsafe church for our family, then you can continue talks with the elders at North Seattle Christian Fellowship."

I said okay. What else could I say? When your wife asks you for a veto vote, there is only one answer. Yes. If I were to say no, then her internal veto vote would automatically activate. The only chance we had to move forward was for her to have equal power in this decision.

I continued talking with the elders, and I developed a seven-step process that either of us could opt out of at any point, starting with an anonymous visit to the church one Sunday. I would then interview each of the elders by survey and write up a ministry prospectus.

If they agreed with the strategy and ministry philosophy I proposed, then they would in turn interview us. If that went favorably, we would present our ministry over a three-week period, ending with an open question-and-answer session.

It would take us eight months to complete this process. I was not in a hurry, and neither was the church. We'd both been burned, and we were being as careful as we knew how.

By June of 1995, we were candidates. We showed up that first Sunday not knowing what to expect. We met with the leaders, both husbands and wives, and they quizzed us about every area they could think of, and I taught on Sunday mornings for the next three weeks. Then we left, and they voted.

In God's grace, my wife had won a free trip to Europe in the summer of 1995. So we were in London when we received a fax from Pastor Richard Vicknair, saying that we'd received a 93 percent vote to come and lead North Seattle Christian Fellowship. I faxed back that we accepted. The spider was back in the game.

We started July 1, 1995. I decided to retain all the staff as I assumed leadership. But as every new pastor knows, you are not the leader just because you have a leadership position. One of my seminary professors, author John Maxwell, said, "Leadership is influence." I had none at this church. Many of the staff had been there twenty-five years, and one had been there thirty-five. I was their 39-year-old skipper who'd been there a month. They were all watching me, and I felt watched.

As I assessed the situation, I began to realize there was a lot of work to do here, and I felt both called and unqualified to tackle this church's realities. Each one of these issues is a minefield in its own right. A separate strategy had to be developed for each one, with a unique timetable as well. Dealing with these issues called for patience, clarity, and focus. I was anxious and confused when I started, but as we cleared each minefield, both my expertise and confidence grew. A few blew up on me, but I managed to survive them. I was becoming better at clearing these land mines before they exploded.

Here are a few of the more significant issues I faced as I prepared to lead a turnaround in this sixty-year-old church.

BUDGET

The budget was adequate as far as income was concerned, about $600,000 for a church of about 300. This gave us an annual per capita giving ratio of just under $2,000 a year for every man, woman, and child, but it was distributed poorly.

Well over 70 percent of the budget was being spent on the staff itself. When the church leaders decided to bring me on, they let no one go; they just added my expense to the total.

This, I discovered, is not unusual in a declining church. No one wants to let anyone go. There is a "reserve and conserve" mentality because the church has already suffered so much loss in its membership. The thought of firing a staff member is emotionally like firing your mother, and no one is going to do that. I would get to make those decisions later, and I knew it.

The church had also put into policy that annually, $20,000 out of missions giving was to be given to congregational families as scholarships toward our Christian school. I was shocked at such use of mission money, and we worked to phase this program out over a five-year period. Nothing was going to happen fast around here.

The church leadership had also struck a deal with the previous pastor, who had served for 30 years (not Vicknair), to pay his retirement. This was the pastor who had led the church into some extensive growth, but also significant pain, through a forced building campaign. Continuing to pay him was a real drain.

We consulted this former pastor to see if he would amend his contract. I explained that the church was in decline and needed any available resources to lead a turnaround. I was hoping he would see the light, that if the church went under, he'd lose everything. He refused to consider any change, and stated so through his attorney.

We consulted an attorney to see if the contract could be cancelled or amended. He said no. We were stuck, and we continue to pay him to this day. As of this writing we have paid out well over half a million in retirement funds to him.

I met with the elders, some of whom had approved this contract with the former pastor, to give them the news. Ed, one of the elders, who was a constant support and a very Godly encouragement to me, and who had lived through every stage of this church for the last thirty-five years, reminded us of the verses in Psalms 15:1-4:

LORD, who may dwell in your sanctuary?
Who may live on your holy hill?
He whose walk is blameless
and who does what is righteous,
who speaks the truth from his heart
and has no slander on his tongue,
who does his neighbor no wrong
and casts no slur on his fellowman,
who despises a vile man
but honors those who fear the LORD,
who keeps his oath, even when it hurts...

We decided to leave this situation to the Lord. As a church we had made an oath to our own hurt. Down the road, God would honor this difficult decision, but at the time it was hard to take.

We decided to go another direction to deal with our finances. One way we addressed the budget issues was through a stewardship campaign. We also eliminated the $20,000 scholarship fund over five years, raised the rent on our Christian school, and took steps to bring our budget into line.

Slowly things began to get better, but the finances were very tight. It felt like we were trying to balance an elephant on a tightrope most of the time. We always had a reserve fund, though. Most of the time it was about $6,000. I calculated that we could keep our church open for about 18 hours if we faced a crisis. Needless to say, financially, we lived right on the edge for years.

FACILITIES

Our total campus at this point was nearly 100,000 square feet, but it was not laid out well and was dated. The campus was very confusing from the moment you drove into the parking lot; it was hard to tell where to go. I used to tell people who got lost on campus that a drunk, demon-possessed architect had designed it. They would laugh, I would feel embarrassed, but nothing would change.

We had three buildings on four acres in North Seattle, which represented seven different construction efforts between 1960 and 1985. Each building had a list of things that needed to be addressed, and of course, there was no money to do anything.

The nursery smelled like mold, the sanctuary literally had buckets catching rainwater during worship services, and dry rot had consumed the studs in the kitchen walls to the point that the sheetrock alone seemed to be holding it up; I am not exaggerating in the least. All of the buildings needed to be painted. Two needed roofs and upgrades to the interiors. The décor made it look like we were living in the 1960s.

To address these needs, we developed two primary strategies, which we enacted over a ten-year period.

First of all, we had several capital stewardship projects, which focused on the main meeting area. Over the years we raised money for new carpet, chairs to replace pews, sound equipment, etc. None of this changed the culture, but it did make us feel better about ourselves.

Leading a turnaround is not only about what you do to move forward; it is also about recognizing what is holding you back and removing those restrictions. Both sides of this equation are important, just as in balancing budgets. You seek not only to increase income but also to cut expenses.

The second strategy was to meet for worship in whichever building we were focusing on refurbishing, so over a ten-year period, we met in all three buildings at different times. We also rented out space, which brought in about 2 percent of our gross income. However, this was often a pain, and we ended up feeling like landlords instead of people on a mission—largely because we were.

The more we worked on our buildings, the more credibility I gained with the established members of our church, which was helpful. I learned that the seniors in our church were more tied into the buildings than any other generation. By working on the buildings, I was embracing one of their core values. They liked that and gradually began to like me.

The opposite was also true: the more we worked on the building, the more frustrating it was to me and to the newer members of our church. It felt like we were becoming more property-focused and less mission-minded.

When a church is property- or building-focused, that is all it sees. In that mindset, the tangible buildings are the church, and since mission is a non-tangible commodity, it is very hard to change perspectives. Most of these older folks were baptized or married here, and many had held their spouse's funeral or their children's dedication in this space. In their minds, it was sacred space and not to be touched except to repair.

It was frustrating to the newer members of the church because they had no connection, memory, or emotions tied to these buildings. They would have had no problem renting a warehouse or school to worship in. I knew this campus focus had to change, but I really felt powerless to change it.

CHRISTIAN SCHOOL

Oh, the joys of a Christian school! Maybe your experience with a Christian school was positive. I know many people have had positive experiences. Mine wasn't.

I inherited a 35,000-square foot building that housed a school with 172 students, 32 of whom went to our church, and 30 teachers, of whom only three were part of our church. It was led by a strong-willed principal, who was also not a part of our church.

Our school was a part of our charter, or constitution and bylaws. The school could set its own budget, and the church was responsible for meeting it. This meant we were in constant fundraising mode to get money to keep the school going. The school and its budget dominated our board meetings for the first few years.

I realized fairly soon that I could possibly lead a turnaround process in the church (the jury was still out on this), but I knew I couldn't lead it if the school remained attached. This turnaround would be impossible if we could not control spending and refocus the church. Everywhere I turned, I was being asked how the school was doing, but I was never asked about the church.

I wanted to scream sometimes, "Don't you realize that if the church goes down, the school is out of business too?"

Within the first year of leading, I came to the conclusion that the school would need to go, but I couldn't say it to anyone. The school had become our reason for being.

I knew this would not be a hard sell to the board because they had already closed our high school the year before I came. The high school was losing $10,000 a month, so the decision to close it, though emotionally difficult, was forced on the church board.

On the other hand, I also knew closing the school would be hard for the congregation to accept because so much of our focus had been on keeping it open. The school was the door to our future, or so this church had been led to believe.

The people had been taught by the previous pastor that the ideal was for a child to grow up in our church, go to our Christian school, marry someone from that school, and produce more children, who would repeat the process. If there were no school, how could this pattern continue?

The obvious answer was that it couldn't, and in my opinion, shouldn't. God did not call us to fortress ourselves from the world, but to invade the world through love and service. The idea that we could have a future as a church by winning lost people never once came up in discussion in the first two years.

I had said during the interview process that I would support the school as long as it paid for itself. But the school paying for itself was never the case, and the church could not continue to subsidize this school. I put an action plan together.

I began to strategically have conversations with key leaders about the school—about its future and how it was connected to the church. I would explain its potential negative impact on our future and how our extravagant support of the school was threatening the church's very existence.

Over the next three years, the leadership community came to the conclusion that the school would have to become its own nonprofit corporation and be responsible for its own financial support, including paying rent to the church for the facilities we provided for them. We established a five-year timeline for this shift to take place. In reflection, this was one of the longest strategic plans implemented.

I learned that taking time to do it right is the fastest way to get things done. In leading a turnaround church, thinking long-term and taking time to work through such decisions is a critical strategy. By 2003, the school was not only fully responsible for itself but was also off our campus and had moved into facilities of its own.

BOARD

When I arrived at the church we had five board meetings a month—yes, five. I couldn't believe it. We met every Friday morning at 6 am to plan the next Sunday's service. Additionally, we met one night a month to review finances for both the church and the school. Making a decision in this environment was laborious.

I was able to eliminate the Friday morning meetings, simply stating that the staff would now take responsibility for the weekly planning of the services. Each of the elders seemed to breathe a sigh of relief, as did I. It was a critical beginning step in creating a new culture at our church.

Our elder board was made up of eight men. Five of them were full time staff members and three were lay people. Having this many staff members on the board made understanding the changes we were making a little easier at the board level, but it also made some things more difficult. As the lead pastor, I was in charge of the staff, but as the pastor, I was also submitted to the board. This made for a very conflicted dynamic.

There was a constant tension in our staff meetings regarding worship. There was also some tension regarding whom to follow, since the former interim pastor, Richard, was now my associate. To alleviate this, I met with Richard weekly to process my recommended changes. This allowed me to gain his support in both the staff and board.

Richard routinely ran interference for me with both the staff and the board for three years. He told me that the Lord had given him the instruction that he must decrease and I must increase, from the words of John the Baptist. He meant simply that his influence must decrease and mine must increase if we were to accomplish Jesus' goals for this church.

There was one more notable issue regarding our church board. During the toughest season of the turnaround experience, 1998–2003, I had an elder resign every January for those six years. I don't think they coordinated it, but it happened that way.

They left for several reasons, but none of them moved away. They all went to other churches in the area. Some left out of clear disagreement with me. Some left because they thought the church should be recovering faster, and others left because the changes were happening too rapidly.

It was incredibly discouraging to experience this, not only for me but also for the staff, the remaining elders, and the church as a whole. When leaders leave, it is often taken as a signal that they do not see the value in the church's direction. Of course, all of these leaders sensed God was taking them away, and I had to simply nod my head in agreement. What choice did I have?

But I learned a secret in those days about how to respond to exceptionally discouraging situations. I learned to wait three days.

When I started to review why an elder made this decision, I sensed the Spirit saying, "Not now. Wait three days." When I knew I would need to announce this decision to other leaders, again the Spirit would say, "Not yet. Wait three days."

It seemed for me that waiting those three days somehow gave me the ability to recover my emotional and spiritual equilibrium. I now wait to respond to a critical email, tough situation, or critical decision for at least three days. Time is an ally. Dwight Eisenhower said, "Take as much time as you can to make a decision, but when you are out of time, decide and move forward."

STAFF

Our full-time staff was made up of an associate pastor, a youth pastor, an administrator, a bookkeeper, a receptionist, and a design and production specialist. Our part-time leaders were in children's ministry and music ministry. I knew we had to focus on children and worship if we were to successfully lead a turnaround here.

Worship is critical because it sets the culture more than any other area of the church. The style of music, the age of the people on the stage, and the leaders in this area all convey church culture. When new people walk through the door, the people they see on the stage are the first ones to tell them if this is a place they can relate to.

Children's ministry also helps set the culture because the cutting edge for any church to grow is people aged 18–35. Many of those are starting their families and want excellent children's ministries.

During this time, I was also able to hire my father as our seniors' minister. It was a decision that really saved my stamina. My dad, a career pastor of over forty years, understood the pain the seniors were going through with all the changes they were experiencing and also understood the turnaround in the church I was trying to lead.

He served as a firewall for me during some of the most critical days. Some of the chronic complainers would come to him, and I would never know a thing about it. He would never tell me unless he thought it was pertinent to the mission. He served faithfully in this position for thirteen years. I know that I could never have led as successfully as I did without his help. He was a true gift from God.

Over the next five years, I was able to transition us into a staff where we had both a full-time worship pastor and a full-time children's pastor, but it was difficult and took five years. Just like every other major change, it was done carefully and prayerfully. Each of these significant changes could trigger a mine, so I was careful to make sure I had as many influential leaders on board with me as possible.

The key transition in shifting the staff came with a major church-planting initiative. Here's how that went down.

I knew as I began leading this church that having the former interim senior pastor become my associate was risky. That risk was minimized due to Richard's sterling character. But I also knew that he had a vision inside his own heart that needed to come out, and he knew it too.

So every six months for three years, I would ask Richard how he was feeling about our progress and what he would like to do in the future. I put no pressure on him, but we both knew that having two senior leaders in the same church was not a good long-term plan. Eventually, there would be a vision clash. Besides, Richard was qualified to serve a church of his own.

At one of these meetings, he said he'd like to plant a church. That resonated in my heart, so we put a plan together to launch a new church in Ballard, a Seattle neighborhood just southwest of us. The elders approved, and we presented it to the church.

I was as supportive to Richard as he had been with me the previous three years, but this church launch was painful for us. I knew Jesus wanted us to do it, but it was risky. When Richard left, we would reduce our staff expense, but then the people who went with him would also take away from the income side. I hoped it would all balance out, but the whole thing was a roll of the dice.

In our first few years, we'd grown from 350 to about 600. As it turned out, a third of our 600-person church went to help plant the new church. That was a big group, but within acceptable guidelines. What happened next caught me by surprise. Being caught off-guard was a feeling with which I was reluctantly becoming more acquainted.

A soldier on the battlefield is always alert and on edge from trying to expect the unexpected; a turnaround pastor must adopt some of those same postures. I was learning to expect the unexpected, and this situation was a prime lesson.

I had assumed that if a third of our church helped plant a new church, then two-thirds would stay and help us with the turnaround. Not so.

What actually happened was that a third went to help plant the new church, and another third voted with their feet not to be a part of the new church plant or to remain with the mother church. It seemed they had not bonded with me or the turnaround purpose we were trying to effect. They simply chose to leave and find other churches.

I was stunned. Within a month, our church of 600 had lost nearly two-thirds, settling in at about 250 people. Launching this church was like a mother giving birth to a 65-pound baby. It didn't kill us, but we were in pain. Any recovery we had gained in the last three years seemed lost.

Looking back, I see that, although painful, it was one of the best things that could have happened to us. Any turnaround pastor knows that just because someone is sitting in church on Sunday, doesn't mean they are with you in purpose and mission. A key part in seeing the vision come forth is removing restrictions.

I was reminded that Jesus taught us in John 15 that both pruning and removal happen for the good of the vine, and that the gardener, not the vine, does the pruning and removal. God had again interfered with my plans. *Intervened* might be a better word. At any rate, I was trying to land on my feet and recover because everyone who stayed was in a state of shock.

This was in 1998. I didn't realize it at the time, but I was about to trip one of the biggest land mines in this church, one that would place my leadership in the greatest jeopardy it had been in up to this point.

I was about to face a tough decision, very much like I'd faced at my former church. This was one of those decisions that keeps you up at night until you make it, then keeps you up for a few more nights afterwards too.

I knew that if I didn't make this staff decision correctly, any progress in our turnaround would be bogged down, and perhaps stopped completely. I also knew that my decision could backfire, and I could be asked to leave. I can't possibly describe how much I wanted to avoid facing that fear again.

I was scared to move and scared not to move. But I was the leader, and Jesus was requiring me to lead. He was telling me to man up and make a decision. The knot in my stomach doubled in size as I picked up the phone to set up the appointment.

◄ 4 ►
A LETHAL DECISION

AS I WAITED FOR MY CALL TO BE ANSWERED, I reflected back on how we'd come to this point.

I had a church administrator, both good at his job and very trustworthy, who had been at the church for twenty-six years. He had served on staff for twenty-four years and had been the treasurer for the last ten years. He had gold-plated character and immense influence.

In my first five years, I had focused the church toward outreach, almost exclusively, because the church was so deficient in this area. My administrator really believed we were out of balance and wanted a stronger push toward discipleship. We disagreed, and the philosophical split was obvious to the leadership community.

About half the board really sided with him, and I knew it. One elder suggested a board meeting without me so everyone could express opinions freely. I refused to comply because, as chairman of the board, I was also an elder and needed to be there to hear what was said. Things were heating up, and I knew it. I'd been here before, and I knew some courageous decisions were going to be required.

It all came to a head in early 2000 when I realized that I needed to let my administrator go. We were simply on two different tracks. I knew that releasing him would set off a series of land mines, but I felt I had no alternative. I met with several of the elders who I knew would support my decision. I wanted their input and advice before I proceeded.

When I met with the administrator, I walked into his office, thanked him for his service, and gave him two weeks' notice that I was letting him go. It was a potentially lethal leadership decision. He was not surprised and replied to my decision with grace, but he said he wanted to know why I was letting him go. We talked for a bit, but the more we talked, the more convoluted it became, as we each went to our own philosophical corners.

So I simply said, "I've made my decision, and that's it." But that wasn't it.

Within minutes, he was on the phone to the supporting elders, as was I. I knew that something would happen, but I wasn't sure what. I had only been at the church five years, and it still seemed like everyone had more influence than I did. I knew that I was spending my last few chips of influence on this decision, but I had to.

The next week I left to do some teaching in South Carolina. I was happy to travel to the East Coast and leave my troubles behind.

At the hotel, though, I received an email from one of my supporting elders, alerting me that the board would be gathering that night to talk about my leadership in my absence. I was also told some of the former elders had been asked to come, but they had refused when they learned I was not going to be there, wisely noting that this meeting would only bring harm to the church.

I knew who was behind this meeting because he had suggested it before, but I had not agreed to it then. Now he was taking advantage of my absence. I appreciated the information, but there was nothing I could do from 3,000 miles away.

I couldn't call my wife for support, knowing this information would only make her worry. We had lived with the knowledge that leadership issues were coming to a head. In a very real sense, we were living month-to-month, not knowing when or if we would be asked to leave. I remember buying a truck and thinking to myself, *Will I be able to make the payments, or will I lose my position before the contract is up?* I hated living in fear, and this elders' meeting in my absence only added to my stress.

There was no one else on staff I could call. Some of the staff members were even waiting to see which way this conflict would go to determine whom they should support. I was about to confront my greatest fear, that of being humiliated and fired—again.

So I decided to drown my sorrows in a steak. I grabbed my Bible and walked across the parking lot to a roadhouse restaurant. I opened my Bible and began to read about Paul. He was someone who experienced and understood conflict, and I was hoping to find both encouragement and direction.

I found exactly what I needed in Acts 27, as though the Spirit were guiding me to this passage. Paul was on his way to Rome to be tried before Caesar. He was on a ship, in a storm that had lasted for two weeks. God sent an angel to Paul to encourage him and promise that all on board would survive if they listened to Paul. Paul gave his shipmates this message:

> *Men, you should have taken my advice not to sail from Crete; then you would have spared yourselves this damage and loss. But now I urge you to keep up your courage, because not one of you will be lost; only the ship will be destroyed. Last night an angel of the God whose I am and whom I serve stood beside me and said, "Do not be afraid, Paul. You must stand trial before Caesar; and God has graciously given you the lives of all who sail with you."*
> *Acts 27:21–24*

What struck me about these verses was the absolute lack of fear on Paul's part. If any person on board should have been afraid, it was Paul. He was under the sentence of death, and there were at least three ways this scenario could lead to his demise. First, the storm could kill him. I've been offshore fishing many times, and I have a great respect for the ocean. Just reading about this storm got my attention. Secondly, Paul was under the sentence of death if he tried to escape. All soldiers on board were under orders to kill any prisoner who tried to escape from the ship. And finally, Paul was on his way to Rome to testify in front of Caesar, where he would eventually be executed for the sake of the gospel—and he knew it.

This was a dead man talking, but he was speaking boldly and without fear. I was afraid to make a decision for fear of being fired. Paul was boldly talking, unafraid of death. The contrast was painfully revealing. I needed to trust God with my future and simply choose to be obedient.

Here is a key lesson I was just beginning to learn about leading a turnaround church: You are always getting ready to make a courageous decision, recovering from a courageous decision, or in the middle of a courageous decision. Many leaders more skilled than I am have used the term *courageous decision*. Making a courageous decision is actually simple obedience and nothing more. Using the term *courageous* makes the leader feel brave, but the bottom line is this: Jesus is asking me to do something. Will I do it or not?

I wasn't thinking about being courageous at all during this time, and I certainly didn't feel courageous. I knew the Spirit was forcing me to face the fears that had held me hostage. This would not be the last time I faced those fears.

I returned home from teaching, and we had an elders' meeting to deal with this issue. Needless to say the meeting was very tense, but the outcome of the meeting was basically good. The administrator would certainly leave, but we would honor and support him in a new ministry endeavor, one he was uniquely equipped to do. We would support him at full salary for the rest of the year, with the salary tapering off the following year. He received 22 months of support in all.

It was a good decision but financially stressful for the church. We now found ourselves supporting two pastors who were no longer part of the daily operation of the church. One was the former senior pastor and the second was our former administrator, who was now launching a new ministry outside the local church. It was unavoidable, and if I had to do it again, I would. But it certainly slowed down any progress we were making.

Years later I met with this administrator, and he actually thanked me for letting him go. His new ministry was very fulfilling. He said that he had been stuck, and my decision had helped him move forward. Courageous decisions don't always turn out this way, but I'm grateful this one did. We have a good relationship to this day.

CULTURE

The next land mine is culture. One definition of *culture* is "the attitudes and behaviors characteristic of an organization." I can tell you in two words what our church culture felt like: leper colony.

That may seem harsh, but it is the best metaphor I can come up with to describe how we felt during those days. I've never been to a leper colony, but my guess is that a leper's best friends are other lepers. That is similar to how we felt as a church. It was summed up in a phrase I heard one day from another church member: "No one new wants to join us, but at least we have each other." That was pretty accurate.

As a result, hardly anyone brought a new person to church. If anyone did bring a guest, the guest picked up on the atmosphere of despair very quickly and usually never returned.

I tried my best to cover my doubts that we would ever change. I was their leader, and I had to keep my game face on. As a result, I would position myself in the lobby each week to connect with people and encourage them. I found myself reverting to my military posture again, moving from foxhole to foxhole, building up the troops.

"Hey, guys, we can do this," I would say. "I know we don't have any ammunition, or food, or support, and we are all freezing and about to be attacked by the enemy. But we will overcome, and we will be victorious." They didn't believe me. I hardly believed myself. But they still kept coming each week.

But in the middle of this discouraging season where it seemed things would never change, there was a small, ever-present promise from Jesus. It was a thought in the back of my mind that never left. It was as if He said, "I'm at work here, in you and in this church. These are tough days, but it will not always be like this." I believed Him.

So I began to adopt the mindset of a church planter myself. I told myself that any church planter who launched with 250 people was doing pretty well, especially if they kept coming each week. That helped a bit, but there was a suspicion inside me that the Lord was not done pruning our church yet. I really hoped He was, but my gut feelings would later be confirmed. He wasn't done.

WORSHIP

Worship is a huge land mine—and by *worship*, I mean *music*, and specifically *music style*. I know worship is much more than music, but for this discussion I want to focus exclusively on music in worship.

My friend, Gary McIntosh, in his book *Three Generations*, helped me incredibly on this subject. Gary and I both worked with the American Institute for Church Growth in the 1980s, and I'd had a chance to visit with him on several occasions about this subject. The basic principle he researched is that we become imprinted with a music style we find personally appealing between ages 15 and 25, and we tend to stick with that music style throughout our life.

Consequently, when my church hit its peak in the late 1980s, it was singing songs largely written in the 1970s, which was normal; churches tend to be about a decade behind cultural music trends. But this was still where we were with our two-and-a-half-hour worship services: singing 30-year-old worship choruses.

As a turnaround pastor, my orders from Jesus were to "give this church to the next generation." That meant I would have to wrestle it firmly, but lovingly, from the hands of the *Builders*' generation (born 1920–1945), skip over my own *Boomer* generation (born 1945–1965), and hand it to the *Busters* (born 1965-1990) coming up behind me. The first step was to hire a worship leader from that generation and give that leader the freedom to recruit and train leaders who would stand with him. I did just that.

Now it is important to understand, as I've said before, that worship defines a church's culture more than any other area of church life, both in turnaround churches and in thriving churches. When new people come into any church, they're looking for people like themselves. Hence, the growth edge of a church, ages 18–35, wants to see their age clearly represented on stage during worship.

Again, this is not to say that we only wanted people of this age in the church or on our worship team. That was not true. We ministered to everyone, and anyone was welcome to participate. But in any church the most fluid group, ready to adapt to change and explore new things, is in that 18–35 age group.

The problem was that the music we had before only attracted older people, and statistically, seniors are the least likely to bring new people with them to church to meet Jesus. We had a huge senior population. In fact 57 percent of our church at this point was age 63 or older. But I knew that if we were going to keep the doors of this church open for another generation, we had to make the mission-based decisions necessary to attract the younger generation.

For the next six or seven years, we focused on this shift, and it worked. It was painful, and I had so many conversations and confrontations about these changes that I can't count them. I was able, though, to hold firm to my decision to shift the worship style because I knew it was key to being obedient, "giving this church to the next generation."

As I look back, I think we are always called to give ourselves away.

Jesus gave Himself away, and the disciples all gave themselves away. Who are we to think that church must be done in a way that only benefits us, especially if it is to the detriment of an entire generation? It is so selfish to think that church is for me, for what I want and what I need. This kind of consumer attitude excludes the mission of Christ's kingdom altogether. We will have to answer for that (I Cor. 3), and that really makes me nervous.

That we must give ourselves away is true in other areas besides worship and music. If you are serving in any area of the church, and you start thinking of it as *yours*, you are about to be disappointed. Jesus wants us making disciples in all areas of the church. That means learning to give *your* ministry away just like He did, so you can continue to grow.

One more point on worship: As we moved into multiple services, we had to decide if we would embrace multiple worship styles. We experimented with this repeatedly for several years. It never worked for us, and it actually further exacerbated the "worship wars." Finally, I simply declared all services would have the same worship style.

I have pastor friends who have successfully gone the other route and developed different worship styles for different services. I have no objections to differing worship styles, but to some degree it simply postpones an inevitable decision. As the service designed for seniors continues, these Godly saints will pass on, and that service will continue to diminish. At any rate, as a turnaround pastor, this is a concept you have to think through.

As a side note, Rick Warren's classic, *The Purpose Driven Church*, has a chapter in it on the history of hymns, including how they were resisted when first introduced into the church. As you read through that chapter, you may notice a parallel to some of the struggle you will have in introducing a new worship style to your church.

MISSION

Mission is the most explosive land mine of all, and here's why: Mission has the power to completely upset everything on a church's agenda—for good reason. If a church is to be missional, it must take its cues from Jesus and not the congregation or the culture. You can see why this is so powerful.

If a congregation believes that the church's primary purpose is to take care of the people who are there, and you as a turnaround pastor introduce the biblical mandate to make disciples, there will be a culture clash. People who expect to be ministered to will now be challenged to do ministry, and this is a major change.

If, however, you help your church understand that its primary reason for being is to accomplish the mission of Jesus by making disciples, then the changes you introduce are seen as progress towards the church becoming more effective in mission.

All churches change, and you as the turnaround pastor are being called to be the primary change agent. In fact, if we are following the Spirit, change is a part of that journey.

Paul taught the Galatians, "If you live in the Spirit, keep in step with the Spirit" (Gal. 5:25). That is strong language for mission-based change, and any kind of change in a declining church raises the tension.

I had learned a valuable lesson in my second church regarding mission and the development of a statement that identifies and clarifies a church's mission. Now I had to put those lessons to work in the development of a mission for our church.

All church mission statements are simply a restatement of Jesus' mission statement to the church in Matthew 28:18–20:

> *Then Jesus came to them and said, "All authority in heaven and on earth has been given to me. Therefore go and make disciples of all nations, baptizing them in the name of the Father and of the Son and of the Holy Spirit, and teaching them to obey everything I have commanded you. And surely I am with you always, to the very end of the age."*

I have discovered that most mission statements are developed fairly quickly, often in the pastor's office by the pastor alone. Then they are run by the other church leaders and given mental assent, as long as he doesn't suggest anything too radical. Church leaders will buy into it, largely because they don't know why such a statement is so incredibly important.

The real value of a mission statement is in the development process, emotional ownership, and execution of that statement. Let me explain.

People own what they help develop. If a church's mission statement is written in the pastor's office, the only one owning it will be the pastor. If, however, a process can be developed that will take the leadership community on a journey of discovery, and they have an opportunity to contribute, then the final mission statement will be a tool that can be used to shape the future of the church. It will also be emotionally owned because everyone had a hand in developing it.

Our mission statement development process worked well for us. From that process we developed a mission statement that we use daily and has worked effectively for nearly twenty years. Here's how we went about it.

I asked all of the church leaders to meet with me one Sunday night per month to help develop a mission statement that would guide us into the future. I knew full well that most of the leaders in that room would not stick with me long-term. I was okay with that, because they were here now. Most turnaround leaders and church planters will go through three complete groups of leaders before hitting their stride.

None of these leaders was planning to leave the church, and all of them had been there for decades. But I knew as we implemented change they would become more uncomfortable, and I had to be comfortable with saying goodbye to them.

In prayer, Jesus told me quite clearly that I must be willing to say goodbye to anyone, rather than try to keep him or her. I believe this posture is essential for any turnaround pastor. Without it, the pastor will be held hostage to anyone's personal agenda just to avoid losing them. At that point the pastor is now letting them set the agenda instead of Jesus.

I am not saying that a pastor should drive people away—and to this date I have asked very few to leave our church—but I know that turnaround churches grow not only because of who comes but also because of who leaves. I had to be okay with that.

We started our process by studying the Scriptures about what Jesus said the church should be doing and the purpose of His church. We conducted it like a small group and always concluded in prayer. Over time, we began to see Jesus' heart for lost people. He was sent to "seek and save the lost" (Luke 19:10), and "whoever will call on His name will be saved" (Rom. 10:13).

It became obvious that the primary purpose of the church was to reach lost people. As a church, we were designed not for ourselves but for people we didn't know yet. This smashed the "church club" idea and opened up the clear notion that our best days were yet to come.

I then asked this group of leaders to tell me phrases that explained the purpose of the church. I listed them on the board, and as I wrote them down, I could see we were getting it. The list of concepts to be included in the mission statement got bigger and bigger, but that was okay. Letting everyone have their say provided emotional buy-in for these leaders. It was all part of the process.

Then I asked the question, "Is every phrase necessary?"

This was critical because a good mission statement must be short enough to be remembered and repeated easily. To further reduce its size, we then asked if every word were necessary, and we replaced long words and phrases with short, impacting words.

After eight months of study, discussion, and debate, we landed on what we believed was pay dirt. Our mission statement read, "Helping people discover, trust, and love Jesus Christ."

It was simple; it was focused; and it reflected Jesus' heart. In addition, it was emotionally owned because everyone had a hand in developing it. This meant the people would sacrifice to accomplish it, so it needed to be a mission worth sacrificing for.

I didn't realize it at the time, but we would use this statement to lend credibility to critical decisions we would make in our future. We still do. Additionally, this statement contained our core values, which would also support both our purposes and strategies.

Our last step was to take this statement to the church for ownership. I did a teaching series on Sundays about the mission of the church. I reminded the church that we would be making a decision at the end of this series on our mission as a church, and this decision represented the direction for our future. The statement we'd developed was overwhelmingly accepted, and I put a check in the win column.

As I reflected back on all I had been through in the last nine years, I was grateful to God, even though I was still discouraged about our lack of growth. It was about this time that I sensed God asking me to fast.

I have fasted from time to time throughout my ministry, but this time it was different. I had God's grace to fast. I simply woke up in May of 2004 and stopped eating. For nine days I ate nothing. I was not hungry. I drank some juice and milk from time to time, but I took no food.

I lost ten pounds, but that wasn't the purpose of the fast. I sensed I was fasting out of obedience, for God to break a stranglehold the enemy had on our church, but I couldn't get more specific than that. As I reflect back, I can see my fasting in 2004 was connected to a sabbatical I'd taken the previous year.

In 2003 I took a sabbatical for about nine weeks to pray and just get out of the ecclesiastical war zone in which I'd been living. Not everyone was happy I took this time away, but God allowed it to happen. I'll always be grateful to the other leaders who carried the weight of ministry during that time.

On my sabbatical the Lord reminded me of our church's past, how we had dominated the church scene in Seattle before our decline set in. As a church of 2,000 people in the 1980s, we were a force for the Kingdom in the area. Granted, we had issues, but still we were a church of mega standards before the word *mega* was commonly used.

During my sabbatical, the Lord reminded me of Paul's word to the Corinthian church (II Cor. 2:11) that we are not unaware of Satan's schemes. As I continued reflecting on this, I sensed the Lord sharing with me a scheme the enemy was using against our church. We were being double-teamed spiritually.

By double-teamed, I mean that our church seemed to have more resistance than other churches of our size. During my time away, I felt like the Lord clued me in to the enemy's marching orders, which were, "It's easier to keep them down than take them down."

When this thought came into my heart, I knew exactly what that meant: It is easier to stop a church from growing than to bring down an effective, already growing church, which is what we once were. From the enemy's perspective, it was better to double-team his enemy now to stop us from growing than to go through the effort to bring us down again, after new growth had occurred.

Now from Christ's perspective, the enemy's plan doesn't mean a thing. Jesus will build His church, and the gates of Hell will not prevail (Matthew 16:18). Period. If resistance is stronger, it may take a little longer, but the church will still move forward. Jesus always wins.

As I continued my fast, I did not know what it would produce, but I sensed something was happening spiritually. Little did I know, or even conceive, that I was about to enter a period of extreme tension, more than any I'd ever been through before. It would also last longer, but it would produce incredible results.

This fast was God's way of preparing me for a new chapter.

INSIGHT FROM LEADERS

Turnaround Church Coaching Network is the tool God used to refocus and help regain momentum in my life personally and in our church. Sometimes a pastor needs a safe place to vent and process; I found my TCCN group to be such a place. In a learning environment of other leaders with like minds, fellowship becomes more than a meeting. It becomes a setting where God can birth and process ideas of great value. The refreshing I receive from the Lord through my cohort is reviving my heart and ministry.

Christian Life Center has experienced growth for several years, yet I knew from a big picture standpoint that we were lacking infrastructure to sustain that growth. A season of plateau and decline followed those years of growth. Being a visionary, I knew the problem, but I had no idea how to find or implement a solution.

TCCN was a lifeline to me and to our church of 700. As John Maxwell said, "I had bumped up against my leadership lid." We have begun implementing what we learned and the results are very gratifying. We have made adjustments in our Sunday service schedule, focused on first impressions for guests, and set in place our assimilation structure with a new whole-campus database and seen our finances trend upward by over 5% instead of the downward trend we'd experienced. We are regaining momentum and moving forward.

When the leader is energized and has the right tools, things can move forward as God intended. We are very grateful.

Pastor Ray Jennings
Christian Life Center
Port Orchard, WA

◀ 5 ▶
LIVING THROUGH EXPLOSIONS

I LOOKED AT THE POSTCARD that I'd just picked up from my mailbox. It was the picture of a local church that wanted to sell its property, and a thought bolted through my mind: *You are to sell your campus and move.* I couldn't get that card out of my hand fast enough. I walked rapidly up to my office, hoping the thought in my mind would go away before I got there. It didn't, and my world started to rock.

At this point, after nine years of leading, I had successfully taken this church from 600 in average Sunday morning attendance to a solid 250 people each week. Oh, the bliss. I had learned to mingle prayer and whining well.

I knew I was not alone. Lots of men and women have led declining churches, but it just wasn't what I was wired to do. I hated the declining attendance, reduced budget, and oversized facilities in obvious disrepair.

During my first three years at this church, I had carried around a growth graph of what our attendance would be with 10, 20, and 30 percent growth over the next five years. I had never considered making a declining graph. What a joke that little piece of work was now.

Jesus created me to lead a growing church, and now He had asked me to lead a declining one. Somehow that made sense to Him, but He was the only one to whom it made sense, which only added to my frustration.

My other pastor friends would ask me at our annual church conference, "How are you doing, Don?" I knew exactly what that meant. They were saying, "How long can you endure leading a church in decline?"

The postcard simply read, "For Sale: Nice One-Acre Parcel—Laurel Hurst Methodist Church." A local church was selling their campus. I didn't know why, and honestly, I really didn't care. That wasn't the problem.

My tension level rose quickly when I pondered the question, "What if we were to do the very same thing?" What if we did what the voice in my heart said to do? What if we put our campus up for sale and sought to relocate? What kind of impact would that have on our church?

The whole idea of selling scared me. Seeing myself standing in front of our church, asking them to sell our 45-year-old, 80,000-square foot, four-acre campus, which many had sacrificed to help build, scared me into shivers.

Such a thought was too painful to consider. Our church was already in pain. We were in pain from too many of my "experiments" as I tried to somehow get this church growing again and pain from saying good-bye to so many friends who just couldn't or wouldn't make this journey with us. We were in pain from having less money than we needed, more property than we needed, very few guests on Sunday, and a very, very uncertain future that no one wanted to talk about. The very notion of selling our campus would simply inflict more pain.

The postcard had grown hot to my touch as I tossed it away, but a still, small voice in my heart said, "Pay attention: something is up here." I knew it was God's voice, but that brought no comfort to me at all.

I booted up my computer and waited for my email to load. I browsed through the rest of the mail, most of it junk, and saw our *Willow Creek* magazine.

As a Willow Creek Association Church, we received a magazine from this incredibly encouraging organization founded by Bill Hybels. I've never met Bill, but like thousands of other pastors, I have often been encouraged and motivated by what he presents.

I thought, *This magazine is just the ticket to get that postcard out of my mind.*

I turned to the first article. It was about a young leader in the Midwest who had led his declining church to grow to nearly 2,000 people. A key turning point was when the congregation decided to sell their campus and relocate.

Internally I screamed, *NO!*

Ambushed again. I had sought relief from the idea of relocating, and instead I ran headlong into it again. I immediately turned the page, looking for a diversion.

The second article was almost identical to the first, except that this pastor had tried to re-engineer his declining church for nine years before introducing the idea of relocating. Now I simply leaned back in my chair and sighed. I could see where this was going. I was caught in a web of obedience. We were moving. The orders had been issued. I wanted to dial U-Haul for a personal vehicle and get out of Dodge.

Every pastor leading a church in obedience to Jesus knows the feeling of making a courageous decision. As I have said before, it is more about obedience than courage. When you have to make one of those decisions, you don't feel courageous; in fact, you may feel like a wimp, wishing the whole situation would go away. That is how I felt, and here's why:

I did not want to stand up in front of this congregation, who had already sacrificed long before I got there, and say, "You know this building where you dedicated your babies, where you married one another, where you had the funerals for your spouses, where you came to a living faith in Christ? Let's sell it."

Even though we had been on this campus for 45 years, the time had come to move, and I knew it in my heart. It was "fish or cut bait." I silently breathed a prayer and surrendered to what I knew was God's will, trusting that He would provide the grace necessary for the people, and me, to accept this new challenge.

I want to say very clearly here that leading a turnaround church doesn't have to involve relocating your church to a new campus. It could, but it doesn't have to. Lots of churches are reborn in the same facilities where they were dying. What it does require is obedience. The key is to listen to Jesus and know His plans. Likely, they will be just as challenging to you as these were to me. But all declining churches will remain stuck unless that pastor leads the church to obey the Chief Shepherd. I take comfort in the fact that Jesus has been leading stumbling pastors like me for twenty centuries.

Over the next month, I began to strategize moving forward. I knew that I needed to meet with Ed, a former board member who still had tremendous influence in the church. He hadn't been on the board for over five years, but influence was influence. And if I ignored that, I would do so to my own peril.

Ed's daughter-in-law, Lynne, a highly gifted woman, had assumed the role of our church's business administrator. She was strong-willed and clearly had a mind of her own, but she really wanted what was best for the church. I knew that if Ed bought into this idea, she would too, so this would be a "make or break" meeting. If I couldn't get two of the most influential people in our church to see the validity of this idea, no one else would buy it either.

It was now September 2004, and at this point in our progress we had transitioned the school off the campus to become an organization of its own. This was a huge victory. We had also concluded two campus upgrades, one costing nearly half a million dollars. Our facilities were looking as good as we could make a structure from the 1960s look.

We had also developed a new culture of focused outreach, implemented a new worship style, aligned our staff with our mission, and embedded the mission in the congregation, but we continued to remain plateaued around the 250 mark. It was painful to say the least. I knew that Jesus was moving us off this campus for the sake of the mission, but I had to play this right or lose the initiative.

The one thing holding us back was this huge piece of property and the simple cost of maintaining it, as well as the emotional ties to all that had happened here over the years. We needed a new start.

At a meeting in September with Lynne and Ed, I proposed the idea of selling the campus based on all the observations I have just listed. It was a defining moment where our church's future was held in limbo as three people talked. I knew that if I presented this idea to the church council, each one of those men would ask if I had also talked with Ed about this, so his support was critical.

We have all been in conversations where we've done our best to lay out the case, looking at every angle, hoping for a positive response. But then we must ask the key question, so I did just that. I looked across the table and said, "Well, Ed, what do you think? Should we consider selling this property and look at relocating?"

I remember his actions very clearly. He looked at me for a moment and said nothing. Lynne looked at him, and then he put his head down. This man had nearly forty years invested in this church, and 90 percent of that time was on the board. He'd lived through every one of the seven church building projects, a regionally known devastating church fight, and also lots of spiritual victories. He'd seen it all.

He then raised his head and said, "Maybe you're right. Maybe this is exactly what we need to do to move forward. I can see some real benefits in moving this direction." I leaned back and quietly sighed. We were on our way.

I knew I still needed to present this to the church council, our board, and then to the congregation as a whole. Then we would need to vote to sell and find a new location, but seriously, all that was just a matter of doing it. I hope that doesn't sound arrogant, but to be honest, the hardest part of the whole process was over. If Ed had chosen to resist this idea, I still would have proceeded out of obedience, but it would have been a much tougher road. I knew that nearly everything in regards to this decision hinged on this conversation right here. Jesus was building some momentum, slowly.

God has given every turnaround pastor influential leaders in their church, and they are very foolish not to listen to them and enlist them as allies, if possible. We are called to lead, not do ministry alone. If no one is following, we are not leading.

I set up a meeting with our church council, and as I expected, they asked if I had talked with Ed. I shared his endorsement, but I wasn't surprised that several of them talked with him independently to confirm his feelings.

With the council's support, we began to strategically leak information out over the next few months about a possible relocation. I met with ministry leaders and other former elders. In October, I announced that we would be having a membership meeting to discuss our church's future, specifically to deal with the question about whether or not to sell the campus.

I was not concerned about announcing it, because all the key players were already on board. If anyone in the congregation had any questions, they would most likely not come to me anyway. They would go to one of the other leaders, who would clearly explain why we were considering this decision.

The value of having other leaders explaining to the people is twofold. First of all, there were simply too many conversations for me to have one-on-one. Like Jethro explained to Moses in the Old Testament (Exodus 18:23), there were too many of the people, and they would simply wear me out. God had given many leaders to do the work, and I would be stealing from these other leaders if I didn't let them do what God had called them to do.

Secondly, there was a huge trust factor involved. Although the people trusted me personally, my position as senior pastor was not fully trusted. The elders had reported to me, and to many other members as well, that the former senior leader, who had previously led them into a building program, had maneuvered in an untrustworthy way. He had pledged a huge offering, and it didn't happen; the project had cost twice what he said it would; and he had promised no borrowing, yet the church was forced to borrow significantly—a debt that I was now helping the church pay off two decades later.

Now I had a picture of what Jesus was doing with the people. He was teaching them to confront their fears as He had taught me to do. I had been afraid of being fired again, and I had to be put in a situation where I trusted Jesus to coach me through overcoming that fear.

This church had been deeply wounded during the last building program, which had been clearly misrepresented to them. They had been told it would cost $1 million, but it cost $2 million. That was not a simple cost overrun. The architect had told the pastor what it would cost, but he had refused to acknowledge it and simply told the church his own figure.

Now Jesus was leading this church to face its fears regarding a huge building project and its mistrust of senior pastors. How much they trusted both Jesus and me would come out in the church meeting we were about to have. I was ready.

The all-church meeting took place in November of 2004, and the room was packed. People who only came to church twice a year were there. I stepped up to the microphone, prayed, and began to speak.

I had 15 pages of manuscript, and I read through my information. I explained why we believed it was necessary to sell the campus. I presented the financial impact. I said some 60 percent of our families, and 40 percent of those in leadership, lived north of us. But the bottom line was that we believed Jesus was asking us to move. Then I opened the floor for comments.

This all-church meeting could have been a series of small explosions being set off all over the church, but I had asked other leaders to weigh in first. The tone of the meeting was set.

I wanted the people to speak too. I knew if we didn't allow people to ask questions, there would be no buy-in, and the vision would stall. This strategy allowed us to avoid many disunity problems down the road. People own what they help create, and these discussions allowed ownership of this process. It took time, but in the long run it was the fastest way to go.

I needed to be the vision-caster, to proclaim the direction and clearly explain why. Then I needed to trust God with each individual conversation. Believe me when I say that it was hard. But it was right, and God blessed that decision not to try to control the outcome.

Finally the conversation, questions, and answers were over. It was time to vote on the question of the night. Will The Northgate Church sell its campus and begin a relocation process?

"Yes," said 98 percent of the people.

Now the vision had legs, or so it seemed. I hoped that such a positive vote meant that we had stopped our bleeding and would now bottom out and start to grow. I was wrong again.

On the heels of this very positive decision to sell and move came another very discouraging season. Over the next three months, a third of our church decided they did not want to be a part of this decision. We dropped from averaging 250 adults and children on a Sunday morning to about 175, adults and children. I was shocked and hurt.

I met with many of these people and asked them, "When we had our church business meeting, I saw you there. How did you vote? Aren't you excited about this new direction?"

They almost all replied with something similar to, "Yes, Pastor, we voted to sell and move. We're excited for you and the church, but we don't see ourselves being a part of this move. We voted to sell because it's good for the church, but it's not for us. Being a part of a building program, raising money, trying to sell this property—it all sounds so stressful. We wish you God's best, but we're not going on the journey with you."

This is so often the case in a turnaround church. Exciting victories are mingled with incredible discouragement.

Nevertheless, we moved ahead, getting a commercial appraisal of our property to find out what it was worth. Up to this point we'd been guessing about the value, and property values were volatile all over the Seattle area during this time. Our four acres came in at just over $9 million, so we explored a plan to sell it, found a real estate agent who specialized in selling and finding church properties, and began to move forward.

I had a meeting with the real estate agent, an elder, and our business administrator. While talking with him about selling our four acres, he told me about a 40,000-square foot Christian college, formerly a public elementary school, on ten acres that he had just listed. We got in a car and drove the seven miles north.

As we toured the campus, I could see the potential, but I also saw that it needed a lot of work to become usable for our needs. The value of this property was there, and the sellers were eager to move it. The downside was that we had no money because we had not finalized the sale of our property. Well, I guess we did have $6,000 in savings. But I felt like the little boy whom Andrew brought to Jesus with the fish and bread. Andrew's brother, Peter, said, "What is this among so many?" But Jesus did a miracle then. Maybe he'd do another one here. He did.

The first miracle was getting us some money to get started. On our four-acre parcel that we were selling, we owned a house that we could separate from our parcel and sell. At our business meeting we had decided to sell it too and use the proceeds to help cover expenses as we researched moving our campus. We had potential money, but no real money.

The following month I told the elders about this new campus, and we toured it together. As we walked through the halls, dreaming and talking, it was clear to me the culture of our church was changing, especially on our leadership team. Jesus was getting us ready.

During the winter I received some important calls that again carried potential for us to move forward. The first call was that we had received earnest money on the house we were selling. Real estate was still going up in Seattle at that time, and the buyer wanted to lock in a price and interest rate. That was good for us. If we could sell this house, we would have at least some money to work with, and we could also catch up on some overdue bills. As a church, we were still hanging by a financial thread. That had never changed.

Let me interject some thoughts on finances here, both personal and corporate, because either one can sink a turnaround process.

PERSONAL FINANCES

If you are leading a turnaround church, chances are you are not going to be making a lot of money. Pastors in general don't make much money, but it is even tighter in a turnaround situation. It is imperative that you get on a budget and stick to it. It will save you incredible heartache if you do. Get Dave Ramsey's *Total Money Makeover* or Ron Blue's *Your Money Matters* to guide you.

Secondly, you must have some kind of reserve fund personally. I know you are laughing as you read this, but I'm serious. For the first six years of our turnaround, our family had no savings and no emergency fund. None. We spent it all to survive, but doing that added to my stress.

When the offerings were low, I was the first one to wait on my paycheck, and sometimes it would be held for a full two weeks. That's painful when you are already living hand-to-mouth. This situation was not short-lived. By that, I mean our family went for over four years not knowing if we would get a regular check on payday. Though it was always received, it would be a week late about half the time.

I took this matter to the Lord, and He gave me a simple idea that you can too. I opened a savings account that I actually used for saving! Amazing! The first goal was to make sure I had enough money to cover one full paycheck. That was my savings goal because then when I didn't get paid, I paid myself from savings. Then when I got my paycheck, I replaced the savings so I'd be ready when it happened again—and it often did.

I know this isn't rocket science, but you'll be amazed at how much peace of mind you can have when there is at least one paycheck in the bank. How did we get the money? Well, honestly, we took a second job hosting foreign students in our home. But there are lots of ways to build up your savings.

If you are leading a turnaround church, I encourage you to set a savings goal and then get after it. Don't buy a burger; instead, eat a sandwich and put the $10 in the bank. Birthday and Christmas gifts go in the bank until you reach your goal. When you start doing this, Jesus will help you. But if you do nothing on this subject, I've found He tends to do the same.

CHURCH FINANCES

There seems to be a unique connection between personal finances and church finances. As you read through Paul's instructions to both Timothy and Titus, he seems to give a signal that an elder/pastor will lead the church the way he leads his family. If that is true, then the way we handle our personal finances will affect how we handle church finances.

Here's what I learned: This is Christ's Church, not mine. He is the owner. I am the manager. He has enough of whatever we need to get the job done, including money. This is a position of pure faith, and although I'd prefer to have the money in the bank, apparently faith is enough. When we are moving forward in obedience to Him, He provides.

That being said, we need to be money-wise, we need to plan, and we need to prepare. But when we've done all we can—and it still doesn't look like enough—and Jesus says to get moving, we get moving.

The price the church had been offered on the house was $185,000, and it was fair. We accepted the purchase offer. This gave us a little money, but we honestly spent over $100,000 of the proceeds of that sale to catch up on church bills and get our campus ready to sell. That left about $85,000 in discretionary funds.

The next phone call I received was from our real estate agent, Bryan, who said a representative was coming to meet us from the organization that owned the property we were considering. He wanted to meet me and talk—no pressure and no negotiations, just a simple meet-and-greet.

I said, "Sure, I'd love to meet him."

The representative's name was Mike, and he was a great guy. He'd been an employee of McDonald's Corporation for years and purchased property for them. He had personally known Ray Kroc, the late owner of McDonald's, and had traveled often with him. He arrived in town the day after Bryan called us, and we went through the campus we were looking at and sat down to visit. He assured me that we were just talking, and then said, "Don, we're selling this piece of property for $5.5 million. It has had over $8 million in upgrades, and there's ten acres here, with four undeveloped. I need to get some sense from you as to how interested you are in this property."

I knew the minute the question was posed that we were negotiating. I had been put in play, even though we weren't supposed to go there. I could have shut down the conversation, but there was also a sense in my heart that I should move forward. This was an opportunity to watch God work, and I was on a faith adventure. Game on! So I responded.

"Well, Mike," I said, trying to sound like a savvy negotiator, "we are interested. The church council has walked over this property, and we think it could be a good home for us. But I'm not empowered to make a deal here today."

Mike responded, "We're not making a deal; we're just talking, but we need to talk specifics to find out your level of interest and to see if this is feasible or not. Are you okay to keep talking?" We had just entered into a non-negotiation kind of negotiation.

I said, "Sure, we can keep talking, and even go into specifics, as long as we both know I'm not signing anything today and everything we talk about is subject to both council and membership approval. Are you okay with that?"

Mike agreed. He continued, "Are you good with a $5.5 million price tag?"

I knew that the first price is the asking price; it's not the real price. I also knew that the Christian financial group that held this property needed to get it off their books, and having a pending sale would help them with an underwriting review.

"I tell you what, Mike. We'll offer $5 million for all 40,000 square feet and all ten acres. How does that sit with you?"

"Let's make it $5.1 and call it a deal," Mike said with a smile and stuck out his hand to shake on it. He was a big man, well over 6'5", and he towered over me. His hand looked huge as he stuck it out in my direction. I looked down and saw my own hand reach out and grab his. As I shook his hand, we both knew the deal was not over, and neither was this conversation.

"Now, what about some earnest money, Don?" Mike asked. "Because that is what will really seal this deal. Are you prepared to put some earnest money down?"

Now I knew that normally earnest money is just that, money that shows earnest, but we didn't have a lot of money to put down. The house sale had not yet closed, so we technically had only our $6,000 in the bank. That was not very impressive, but I wasn't going to tell him that.

In a commercial deal like this, 10 percent or more would be expected as earnest money. I was about half a million short, but there was a boldness that came over me at this moment. I don't know how to explain it; I simply became very bold. I know looking back on this scene that it was the Spirit working in me. I wanted to know if God was in this or not, so I would do all I could. If that were not enough, then I wanted to find out early in the game.

"Sure, Mike, we're ready to put some earnest money down," I said as confidently as I could muster. "We'll put down $50,000 within two weeks."

Mike leaned forward in his chair and said, "You're offering to put down $50,000 on a $5 million piece of property? That's all?"

There were two other people in this discussion: Bryan, the real estate agent, and Lynne, my business administrator. They both turned and looked at me. I knew my response was key, but the boldness had not left.

I maintained direct eye contact with Mike and replied, "Exactly. We're offering $50,000 earnest money within two weeks. If you accept that, I will take a $5.1 million deal to the church council and then the membership for approval, pending the sale of our old campus. Do we have a deal?"

Mike smiled and said yes. They needed this sale as much as we needed to move. What a moment. That short twenty-minute conversation concluded our non-negotiation-negotiations. Now all we needed to do was sell our campus. That would be simple, right?

About a month before this decision, shortly after we'd gone public about selling our four-acre campus in Seattle, we'd been approached by another church. We'd rented a portion of our campus to them for over seven years. It was an international church, and their pastor, Chris Chan, asked to meet with me to talk about purchasing the campus. I knew a $9 million price tag would be steep for this college-age church that had only existed for ten years. I also knew I had to have this conversation, but I was pretty sure it would end with disappointment on his part.

Chris sat across the table from me in my office. I had enormous respect for this man, who had built a church of college-age students, most of whom were with him only four years while they were getting their education at the University of Washington. He opened the conversation and asked, "Don, what is the selling price on the campus? I think we may be interested in buying it from you."

"Well, Chris," I responded, trying not to disappoint him too much, "we're selling it for $9.2 million. That's quite a stretch for you guys, I know."

He was more ready for my response than I was for what he was about to say. He said, "Pastor Don, ten years ago when we started our church, we set a goal for each student who came. We asked them to donate one dollar a day to a future building for our church. For ten years we've been receiving about $30 a month per person, and we have $2 million ready to put down on this property."

Now it was my turn to be shocked. WOW! What sacrifice and forethought this young leader had. I was amazed. These students, knowing they would probably never be able to see a building, gave regularly anyway. I was very impressed.

"Chris," I responded, "I'm shocked. You really have $2 million to put toward this purchase?" He assured me that was the case. I said, "Okay, I'll take this offer to the council, and we can draft an earnest-money agreement. How much are you ready to put down for an earnest-money agreement?"

Remembering the conversation I'd had with Mike about the property we wanted to buy, I was ready to be very understanding. Chris looked at me and replied, "We're ready to put down $500,000 as earnest money today."

And with that our campus was sold. Now that doesn't mean we got our money. An agreement is not a check, and this would turn out to be a very complicated and drawn-out real estate deal. I have been in real estate deals in every church I've pastored, and nothing I had experienced had come close to what I was about to encounter.

There were three groups involved in this real estate transaction: our church, the international church Chris led, and the Christian financial group that held the paper on the property we were trying to buy.

We agreed to sell our property to Chris for $9 million. He put $2 million down and applied for a loan for the remaining $7 million, but he didn't qualify. The church had not been in existence long enough for such a note, and they didn't have the cash flow to service the loan. This financial minefield looked like it was going to blow this deal apart. A motivated buyer without money to buy the property means no sale.

At this point, the Christian financial group we were buying our property from stepped up and said, "Don, the sale of our property to you is very important to us, and we are a lending institution, so we will lend Chris $2 million to move him forward on the deal."

That was amazing! That's as if you're trying to buy a house from someone, who's buying a house from another person, and that third party then loans you money to buy the house you want. When does this happen in the real world?

I'll tell you when: when there is a high level of trust—and a little desperation too. All three of us were working toward the same goal.

But that meant that Chris and his church were still $5 million short. The only way this deal was going to happen was if our church carried the note on that remaining amount. So we agreed to carry the $5 million for the international church, providing they rented the 35,000-square foot school building within a few months. The goal was for them to rent the additional space, show the bank some solid increase in cash flow, and thereby qualify for a loan that would in turn be used to pay off their debt to us, as well as their debt to the Christian financial group.

It was a financial domino game, but it was working. The deal moved forward, Chris paid us $2 million; we paid fees and half a million on our new property and kept back about $800,000 to start remodeling our new campus. After all, this deal was going to be wrapped up in six months, right? Assuming a campus rental for Chris really happened, which everyone thought would be fairly easy. This would increase cash flow and qualify them for a note, and then everyone would be paid off. It was so simple in our conversations.

But it was not simple. Chris was able to rent the school building, but it did not bring in the cash flow we all needed. So the bank would not approve the $7 million loan. Now we were stuck financially.

We were making our interest payments to the Christian financial group as long as Chris made his interest payments to us. Chris was also paying the Christian financial group each month. It was a financial circus. As it turned out, we would have to wait years for our money, not the six months we all thought.

The three-year contract we had with Chris for a full payoff would long expire, but God did come through. I came to the conclusion that

God did not read the contract we signed, or He didn't feel obligated to cooperate with our timetable. With each little setback, I was actually becoming more comfortable with my unfulfilled expectations. God was really in charge, and I was learning to rest in Him. I'll give more details later on how this worked out.

Let me share with you how we danced through another minefield as we continued to move forward in our turnaround process.

I loved our seniors, and they loved me. But seniors, of any group in the church, have the most affinity with the building. I knew I needed to meet with them, to walk through the process and let them ask me any question they wanted. I also knew that if we didn't have their support, this whole strategy could easily be torpedoed, and that would be that. So I asked my father, who was serving as the seniors' minister then, to set up a lunch.

I arrived for the lunch at my mom and dad's house, walked through the door, and immediately felt the icy atmosphere. You would have thought I was there to repossess a family's baby for not paying their hospital bill. This group knew me, and I knew them. I'd been their pastor for nearly ten years, but no one would talk with me in this meeting or look me in the eye.

I sat down at a nearby table to eat and make some light conversation, but to every question I asked, I received only one-word answers. Talk about a hostile environment. I knew I needed to be ready for this. I prayed silently for wisdom and patience.

I knew this wasn't personal, that they didn't hate me, but this major change in our church was destabilizing to them. And I was the one leading this change. The whole atmosphere was clearly described in one sentence by one of the senior ladies.

She said to me personally before the meeting began, "If you tell us we're going to sell our church, I'm going to burst into tears." The whole room heard her say this, and just like that, I was in play.

I responded, "Well, we do have an offer, and we are looking at another campus. But nothing is firmed up yet, so let's talk about it, okay?"

So we sat down and talked. I shared with them about the postcard, my conversations with Ed (the influencer) and Bryan (the real estate agent), and about the new property. With each new topic I repeated the statement, "Could this be God leading us?" This phrase clearly represented what was in my heart. I didn't know it at the time, but God would use that short statement to break the icy atmosphere in this meeting.

Then the time came for questions. The man who had given me cold, one-word answers raised his hand to speak and started in.

He said, "At each point in this story you've just told us, you asked, 'Could this be God'. And now you're inviting us to walk on this journey with you. This is not what I expected when I came here today."

I was surprised and asked, "What did you expect today?"

He answered, "Our church history has always been where the pastor says, 'This is what God wants us to do, so get on board or get out of the way.' But you didn't do that. You are asking us to pray with you and discover God's will alongside you. That is much more inviting, and I'm ready to do just that. I think we all are. Everyone here really wants God's will."

Wow! I had just stepped over a mine that easily could have been set off. If I had pushed this, instead of trusting God, I would have created resistance instead of alignment. This took no skill on my part, and I was very grateful to the Spirit at that moment for His help.

Suddenly, our seniors opened up. Questions started popping around the room, and the atmosphere totally changed. Now everyone wanted to know all about this possibility. The excitement began to grow.

After about 20 minutes, I asked, "Would you like to go see our possible new campus?"

Everyone said yes, and off we went, driving the seven miles in five different cars. We walked over all 40,000 square feet, and the dream was born, not just in my heart but in theirs as well.

At the business meeting to accept the offer, almost every one of these seniors stood and voiced support for this move. I was amazed at how God worked this out. God was clearly working in our church and in our hearts, and it was noticeable. He had already done some amazing miracles, but there were more to come.

I didn't realize that some of the most personal, powerful, and painful chapters lay ahead. But they would also contain some of the most meaningful times, allowing Christ to change hearts deeply, starting with mine.

And then there was the money. How and when would we ever get the money?

◄ 6 ►
HEART CHANGE

I THOUGHT GETTING THE MONEY from the sale of our property was the biggest challenge ahead of us, but that was not the case. While we would get paid, it would be a long, drawn-out, and faith-building process. But before any checks were delivered, there was something else Jesus had in mind.

One key truth I've learned at just about every juncture in leading a turnaround church is, whatever problem you're facing is more about you and Jesus than you and the problem.

This is not to say we don't face real problems—we do. But my tendency, and I'm guessing yours too, is to concentrate on the external problems and ignore the internal issues.

Whatever problem you're facing is more about you and Jesus than you and the problem.

It was significantly easier for me to focus on facilities, or finances, or staff issues, rather than deal with the hurt and fear in my own heart. What I didn't know is that those internal issues were much more powerful at holding our church hostage than any of the external issues I mentioned in the previous chapter.

Jesus was setting me up to deal with a huge problem in my own life. It wasn't a sin issue, but it was an obedience issue, which of course could turn into a sin issue if I didn't obey.

I thought we were off and running with the new objective of relocating our campus, so I set out to help get us moving. Now it was time to build momentum with the leadership community of our church. I had already held a series of meetings with the elders, and the staff was on board too. Now we needed to expand the circle by bringing our ministry leaders into the mix.

So we set up an informational meeting with our full leadership community. We brought in our real estate agent, Bryan, to talk about the move and why it was a good idea for our church. Bryan was proving to be much more than a real estate agent. He was a Godly man who had taken a genuine interest in me personally and in our church in general.

Later on, after the deal was done, he would confide in me that this was the most complicated church real estate deal he had ever done and the most spiritually resisted move he'd seen a church make. Considering the many church real estate deals Bryan had helped conclude, that was saying something.

We also brought in our architect to comment to our leaders on what changes needed to be made to the new building and approximately how much it might all cost. The architect, John Taylor, was a gifted man and had at one time been a significant leader in our church. He had opted not to make the journey with us and had left during my fourth year as pastor. But we remained good friends, and he was committed to helping us be successful. He did a splendid job for us. It really does us no good to burn relational bridges in the Kingdom.

At this leadership meeting I presented first, casting vision as best I could on how we would proceed. Then Bryan presented the case for how this would benefit our church, and finally John presented the estimated costs of such a move. Now it was time for questions.

One of our current elders, Rick, stood to make a comment. I could see by the expression on his face he was nervous about what he was going to say to the group.

I'd been deeply involved in spiritually apprenticing Rick over the past three years, and I'd watched him grow in Christ. I had a gut feeling his nervous expression meant he was going to say something that would bring added tension to our discussion. I trusted Rick and knew that if it needed to be said, he would say it well, so I listened carefully.

Rick started in, "Originally, I was against this move. It seemed to me that we were just changing locations with a hope that such a move would solve our problems. I know the move alone won't solve what we're dealing with, but I am no longer against this move. In fact, I think we should make this move."

Rick waited a moment, then continued, "But I still believe that simply changing our address will not solve our problems. This is a heart issue: our church needs a new heart, and only God can give us a new heart. I don't know how He will do it, but I do know I need it and I think we all need it. We need to become a church that cares more about others than ourselves. I think this campus move is part of the change we need, but I think we need the heart change more than a different piece of real estate."

His words echoed through my heart: "We need a new heart." Have you heard a phrase you couldn't get out of your head? That's what was happening to me.

I totally agreed with Rick. We needed a new heart, but how could that happen? How could hundreds of people get a new heart? How could I get a new heart? It became a resonating prayer from deep within, "Jesus, please give me a new heart."

That following week, I had a breakfast meeting with a missionary we supported in Eastern Europe, John Krueger. John is about twenty years older than I, and he is what I imagine the Apostle John to have been like. He has that kind of gifting, to start something substantial in forgotten places and watch it blossom.

John and I had traveled in several European countries together, training local pastors, and we had become very close. I trusted him, and he knew it, which is what allowed him to speak into my life like he was about to.

After breakfast he spoke up, "Don, we've traveled a lot together, and I've watched you teach pastors in a variety of settings. You are gifted and know leadership like very few pastors I know."

I felt like I was being set up, but because I trusted John, I didn't interrupt. I wanted to get it out on the table and hear the whole thing before responding. I did know, though, that whatever he said would be somewhat painful. It seems that a pastor's ability to grow personally is directly connected to the level of pain he is willing to embrace. I didn't know it at the time, but I was about to go on a little journey of embracing pain myself. It would prove very profitable and change the trajectory of the rest of my life.

John continued, "But I have to say, there seems to be a disconnect between your head and your heart. You can spout statistics and ratios and cite studies and produce graphs, but all that is head knowledge. It's helpful, but it's cerebral. There's little heart in all of that. There is a sense that your heart and head are disconnected. Does that make sense to you?"

"Well, John," I said, "I understand your words and the concepts, but I'm not sure how to apply it. I have to be myself. That's how I think and how I process. It's just who I am."

I was defensive in my response, and I knew it. I didn't want to put him off, because this kind of conversation was a little out of the ordinary for John. I could see he was uncomfortable putting me under pressure. But it was like he was on an assignment to get through to me, and he wasn't likely to let up.

Honestly, it never occurred to me that this conversation could be connected to the prayer I'd been praying for Jesus to change my heart. I never put the two together. I'm sure Jesus did, and I'm sure you, the reader, can see the obvious connections. But that's the nature of deception. The deceived person doesn't know they're deceived until someone else tells them. That's exactly what John was trying to do.

John continued, "Don, have you read John Eldredge's book *Waking the Dead*? I think you would enjoy it, and it would help you understand what I'm trying to say from a different perspective."

"No, John, I haven't read that book," I said, slightly frustrated at the thought that one more book could really make a difference in my life. "John, if I read every book that people recommended to me, I'd do nothing else. I know you know what I mean."

He replied, "I understand. I just felt like I should mention it to you."

And that was the end of our conversation. I appreciated all John was trying to do for me, but I was really not interested in reading another book. Reading is hard for me, as I'm a little dyslexic, and if I can skip a book or listen to it, I'd rather do that.

I headed back to the office, totally forgetting about the breakfast conversation with John, and I immersed myself in work. I had several meetings that morning and then checked my schedule. I was meeting our real estate agent, Bryan, for lunch that day, so I headed out to see him.

By the time I got to the restaurant, Bryan was there waiting. Bryan was a tall, 60-something man with a winning way about him. He knew people and churches and was good at his job. He stuck his hand out to me and said, "Hi, Don, good to see you. I think they have our table ready."

"Good to see you too, Bryan," I replied, genuinely meaning it.

Bryan had been a source of incredible encouragement to me as we walked through this chapter together. He had already helped negotiate some tough situations, and I had come to trust him, both as an agent and as a brother.

We finished lunch with small talk about our recent fishing trip and churches, and then he moved to what he really wanted to talk about. The look on his face became very serious, and he leaned forward. I could tell he wanted me to get whatever he was about to say.

He jumped in. "Don, you and I have been walking through this together for nearly a year now. We've fished together, and you and I have done leadership seminars together several times. I feel like I've come to know you during that time."

I felt like I was being set up for the second time that day. What was coming around the corner in this conversation? I had no idea, but I did trust God and Bryan. So I chose to be open, even though I knew there was again going to be some pain involved. I was a little nervous; I could have let fear shut my heart down, but I distinctly remember making the decision to keep my heart open.

"I feel like God has put something on my heart I need to tell you," Bryan continued, "and I'm not sure really how to say it. So I'm just going to jump in."

"Sure, Bryan, go ahead. I trust you, and I'm ready to hear whatever you have to say to me," I said, trying to sound authentic, but still a little nervous.

"Don, you are one of the finest leaders I've seen," Bryan said, "and you know and understand leadership well. But as I have watched you lead your people through this season, it seems to me that your head and your heart are disconnected. It's as if you are leading out of your head. Your people need to feel your heart, and they're not.

"Have you ever read a book by John Eldredge called *Waking the Dead*? It is the best book I know of to help you understand what I'm trying to say, and if you haven't read it, I think you should. I believe it will be a great help to you. Would you consider reading it?"

I could not believe my ears. Were these guys reading from a script? As God is my witness, these two men said the same thing, with nearly the same words, within four hours of each other. I felt like I was being set up. I knew that Bryan didn't know John, but I just had to find out for sure. So instead of responding to his question, I asked one of my own.

"Bryan, do you know John Krueger?" I blurted out.

"No, who is he?" Bryan asked, a little perturbed that I had not answered his question, which he had been nervous about asking in the first place.

I answered, "John Krueger is a missionary from our church. He had breakfast with me this morning and said to me virtually everything you just said to me about my head and heart, including mentioning this same book. I'm stunned. I can only conclude that God wants me to read this book."

Bryan got a big smile on his face and said, "I agree, Don. God is talking to you through us, and I do think you should read it."

I left that restaurant, went straight to the bookstore, bought *Waking the Dead*, and began reading immediately. Now this book did not give me all the answers I needed—in fact, it raised a few more questions—but it was very helpful.

Waking the Dead is all about the heart. The author, John Eldredge, goes into great length to teach us that our human heart (not the organ) is filled with evil before we come to Christ (Jer. 17:9), but after we are redeemed, God fills our heart with good things. Jesus said that a good man, out of the good treasure of his heart, brings forth good things (Matt. 12:35).

As I look back on how God brought Eldredge's book into my life, I see it was clearly part of a sequence He was putting together. Reading this book was designed to get me started thinking about my heart, and it did.

Many of us live with dead hearts spiritually. And I had to admit that mine was dead too, meaning I was disconnected from real life with Jesus. I was born again, and I'd go to heaven if I died. But I was disconnected from the adventure with Him. I was alone in this fight, and my self-esteem was on the line.

I remember praying as I read through Waking the Dead over the next few weeks, and Jesus spoke to me in my heart so clearly. He said, "Don, if your church never grows past 150 people, and I want you to stay here for the rest of your life, would you do that if you knew your obedience put a smile on My face?"

This was a test of my shepherd's heart. Would I respond to the Chief Shepherd appropriately, and would I care for my sheep appropriately?

Now here was Jesus, the leader of the Church, who wanted His Church to grow, asking me if I would lead a stagnant, plateaued church for His glory.

I could only say yes, but it was at that moment I deeply realized I wanted our church to grow for the wrong reasons. I wanted to feel good about myself, because I was leading a growing church. I wanted others to look up to me. It was all about me. What an ugly heart I had, and what an ugly revelation this was. My heart was a mess. As discreetly as I could, I burst into tears right there in the restaurant where I often read and wrote.

I felt like I had been found out. I could no longer hide my heart from myself. Interestingly enough, it was at this moment of both revelation and repentance that Jesus was very real to me, encouraging me to go forward, as if this revelation of my spiritual incompetence actually made me more credible, even more competent to lead.

It has always amazed me that the more authentic we are with both the Lord and ourselves, confessing our weakness and frailties, the stronger we become (II Cor. 12:9).

As I lifted my head from prayer and wiped the tears from my face, I felt this strange sense of destiny. God was working in my life. I was not alone. My heart was being affected, but I knew in my gut that this short period of repentance and awareness was not enough. There was more to come, but I had no idea how deeply God would work on my heart. I knew that this meant dealing directly with my fears and resistance, and I was nervous.

As I reflect on this process, I've concluded that for a church to experience a turnaround externally, it must begin internally, in the heart of the pastor. Then the people in the church and finally the community will notice the change. As I look back, I see I was in a personal turnaround so deep it is difficult to contemplate.

As I continued to pray, "God change our hearts," I started asking if there were any story in the Bible that reflected how God had changed the hearts of a group of people. Specifically, I wondered, how did He do that? As I pondered this question, the story of Moses surfaced.

God had changed the entire nation of Israel's heart. They had been a nation of two million slaves, and somehow they became a mighty army. Now changing Israel into an army was a process, a bumpy process at that, but it had happened nevertheless. I thought there could be something I could glean from this narrative.

I started reading about the life of Moses in Exodus, and in chapter three I had an eye-opening experience. I'm sure you've had the experience of reading a familiar passage in the Bible and seeing something you'd never seen before. That's exactly what happened to me.

In Exodus 3, we find Moses tending the flock of his father-in-law, Jethro, who was a priest and would gain influence in Moses' life. Moses saw a burning bush that was not consumed. He investigated further, and God called out to him.

> *When the LORD saw that he had gone over to look, God called to him from within the bush, "Moses! Moses!" And Moses said, "Here I am." "Do not come any closer," God said. "Take off your sandals, for the place where you are standing is holy ground." Then he said, "I am the God of your father, the God of Abraham, the God of Isaac, and the God of Jacob." At this, Moses hid his face, because he was afraid to look at God.*
> *Exodus 3:4–6*

Now this was the place where God began to work on Moses' heart. If God were going to change the heart of a nation, he would have to start with the leader. He would have to deal with the leader's fears and insecurities in order for that leader to become what God wanted him to be.

You'll notice that in Exodus 3:6 in the NIV, God first identified Himself as the "God of your father," and then He identified Himself as the God of the three patriarchs. I have always put an *S* after the word *father* in that verse, but there is no *S*. It doesn't say *fathers*; it says *father*. God is referring to Moses' literal, earthly father, Amram (Ex. 6:20).

Now this is distinctly different than later in the chapter. In verse 15, when Moses asks God, "Whom shall I say has sent me," God replies this time using the word *fathers*.

> *God also said to Moses, "Say to the Israelites, 'The Lord, the God of your fathers—the God of Abraham, the God of Isaac, and the God of Jacob—has sent me to you.' This is my name forever, the name by which I am to be remembered from generation to generation.*

I am not a Hebrew scholar. I am a local church pastor who looks to God's Word, the Bible, for guidance. But when I saw this Scripture,

I was deeply moved, and here's why: Amram was obviously a man of courage for God to bring him up in this conversation, and Moses had undoubtedly met his own father at some point, or at least heard about him from his mother.

When Moses was born, Pharaoh had issued an edict that all male babies born to Hebrew women should be killed (Ex. 1:16), but Moses was spared this tragedy, because his courageous parents hid him for three months (Ex. 2:1–2). The story continued with Moses' mother, Jochebed, making a small basket and floating him down the Nile River in front of the princess. Moses was then rescued, his life spared, and his mother selected from the Hebrew slaves to raise him.

Now somewhere in all this mix, Moses' father, Amram, had to play a role, and although I can't prove it, I think Amram's courage was a big part of this story. He was part of saving Moses' life also, helping to hide the baby for the three months.

Amram would've had to face his own fears and deal with defying the orders of Pharaoh. He as much as said, "No one is getting my son—not on my watch. God gave him to me, and I'm going to protect him."

Now when God brought this up to Moses at the bush, he was reminding Moses of how his earthly father faced his own fears regarding Pharaoh. Moses would have to do the same.

Remember, Moses was in the desert, running from Pharaoh for having killed an Egyptian, and if he returned to Egypt, which was exactly what God was asking him to do, his life would become very uncomfortable. God wanted Moses to face down his own fears, return to Egypt, and let God use him to set His people free. This is perhaps the greatest turnaround saga in history.

As I read this story, I knew God was asking me to face my fears too. I could not help our people move forward in facing their fears without facing mine. I could not lead them in a congregational heart change without first changing my own. In that moment I knew exactly what Jesus wanted me to do, and I wanted to throw up.

Simply put, my greatest fear was being fired again, and Jesus was asking me to deal with it. I was going to have to learn to deal with fear again and again, just like Moses did. Now I'm not putting myself in the same category as Moses; I'm just saying leaders have to deal with fear.

In fact, if there is a fear a leader is unwilling to deal with, that becomes the very fear that holds the leader hostage.

Specifically, Jesus was asking me to visit as many of the 15 elders who had left our church during the previous ten years and ask them three questions. I was to take notes and listen and learn, and I was to do it right away, within the next two weeks.

Now I can't tell you how I knew this, but there was a clear sense that if I didn't do it, I would be disobedient. That sense alone was enough to propel me into action. I made a list of all 15 and made arrangements to meet with 14 of them. The last one had moved out of the area and was unavailable.

No one knew I was meeting with former elders. I did not share it with the church council or staff. Even my wife and family had no idea. I wasn't trying to be slick; I just didn't know how it would all turn out, so I was keeping very tight-lipped about this whole process. Even in obedience, fear played a big role in my life.

The three questions I was to ask were:

1. What did you gain by leaving our church?

2. What observations do you have about my leadership?

3. Why do you think high-quality leaders leave our church?

The responses I got from the former elders were revealing, painful, and encouraging. Most of the leaders were kind, but a few took the opportunity to take some shots, which I'd expected.

Here are some of the comments I heard during the interview process, as it related to my pastoral leadership. I've taken them word-for-word from the notes, which I still keep as a reminder of what I learned.

"You were very controlling."

"You seemed to be dominated by fear of other leaders."

"You had a leadership agenda that would not be adjusted."

"When someone disagreed with you, you reacted defensively."

"We didn't feel like we had permission to bring up some subjects at the elder level that needed to be talked about, so my only options were to live in frustration or leave the church, and not wanting to be a troublemaker, I chose to leave."

After about ten days of such conversations, I felt worn out, but there was also a sense that Jesus was pleased I was willing to look at my dark side. Every pastor has a dark side, and we like to keep it hidden from others and ourselves. It is only when we are forced to see it through circumstances, or we choose to expose it in order to be obedient, that we really grow. For me, it was a combination of both choosing to be obedient and being forced by circumstances.

I knew God wanted to change my heart, and before I could allow Him to do that, I had to see how ugly and dark my heart really was. Honestly, I have listed only a few of the comments above because it is still painful to review my notes from those interviews. God has changed my heart, but it is a dynamic process that continues to this day. I'm glad we don't have to have it all together for God to use us.

In spring of 2005, I presented a four-part teaching series on the heart, and I invited each of the former elders to join us for the first Sunday of that series. Ten of the 14 elders I interviewed decided to come that first Sunday as I taught on "Open-Heart Surgery" and used the story of Moses to convey openly what God had been teaching me.

As the former elders all came in, some with their wives, the level of shock began to rise in the congregation. They all wondered what was up. Hadn't all these men left our church? Why were they all here today? I let the tension rise for a while, and then I addressed it as a part of my sermon.

I said, "Some of you have noticed that we have a group of former leaders here today. They have come at my invitation. Each of them are now part of other fine churches, but they came today to help me address my fears."

I then shared with the church what God had shown me from His Word about Moses dealing with his fear, and that God cannot change a group without first dealing with the leader. I confessed that my greatest fear—working with other church leaders—had affected my relationship with these men. I said I had met with each of them for both reconciliation and to ask them some personal questions about my leadership and how I could grow.

Then I turned to the congregation and openly confessed to them. I said, "My fear has not only hindered my leadership at the elder level. Many of you have felt it too. There has been a level of duplicity to my leadership as your pastor. On one hand, I have welcomed you to come into relationship with me," I continued, "But on the other hand, I have held you at arm's length, not wanting to get too close."

I wrapped it up by saying, "I know our church needs heart surgery, but before I can ask you to let Jesus work on your heart, I have to let Him work on my heart, just like God worked on Moses' heart before He worked on Israel's. So today, I am asking you to forgive me for not letting you into my heart and for holding you at arm's length. I am asking you to pray for me as God does spiritual surgery on my heart as a part of preparing us for the next chapter He is taking us into."

The congregation responded so well. I felt like we had turned a corner. By making my private fears public, and bringing them out into the open, I had given the church permission to talk about the fears they were dealing with. God was really doing surgery on our hearts.

That day was April 9, 2005. I will never forget that day or the sermon on "Open-Heart Surgery" because God has an incredible sense of humor, which we usually enjoy after the fact. You see, the next day was April 10, and I was scheduled for my annual routine treadmill test with my cardiologist for a weak heart valve. While on the treadmill, just as I was working up a good sweat, I saw Dr. Haines lean forward and look at the monitor.

He said, "Uh-oh." That is never a good sign.

He explained that part of my heart was enlarging, trying to compensate for another part of the heart that wasn't working well, due to the leaky valve. I would need surgery soon.

At age 49, and within 24 hours of preaching on "Open-Heart Surgery," I was scheduled for open-heart surgery. Now God really had my attention. On the drive home I think I heard Jesus chuckling, but I'm not sure.

The surgery went fine, but my physical heart would become a living metaphor for the process our church was going through. Following the surgery, I had an infection that plagued me every three months for the next five years. It eventually cleared up, but it was a living reminder that God was still working on me and still working on our church.

It was almost as if the healthier we got as a church, the healthier I got personally, or vice versa. I'm not sure. As God changed our church culture and removed more of the toxins from our environment, the bouts of infection surrounding my heart lessened. It felt like I was living out our church's changes in my body.

Interestingly, it was about this time that our people began to bring their friends to our church. For the first time in over two years, we had new people visiting our church, and some of them were staying. There was a sense that we were actually moving forward—slightly. But hey, forward is forward. Our optimism was beginning to rise.

I wasn't the only one to face personal and physical issues during this time. During the relocation process of our church, we faced some major leadership setbacks and obstacles.

Out of seven elders, five of us spent time in the hospital over the next year and a half. Some were in the hospital for sickness, one fell off the roof of his house, and a moving car in the parking lot hit another elder. It was a little weird, but in each case there was a divine note: God did not spare the pain, but He provided amazing grace for protection, recovery, and even blessing.

The remaining two elders each faced challenges of a different sort. One was removed from serving and faced public discipline for a sexual ethics violation. The final elder and his wife, who was on staff part-time, left the church due to conflict.

Anytime a church chooses to move forward, there will be conflict, because we are in a war. There are obstacles to face, but God will see you through them. There is no reason for fear. It is much like Paul said, "A great door of effective work has opened to me, and there are many who oppose me." (I Cor. 16:9).

It seems that God has a priority when it comes to heart change. If the leader is unwilling to face a heart change, the process stops there; but if the leader is willing, then God moves into changing the leadership community. Then God moves into the people, changing their hearts individually so He can use them to change hearts beyond the church walls.

During this season, we saw our church begin to grow and break through 200 in attendance with only one service. It was exciting to see new people come to Christ and see established people begin to reignite their faith. I will never forget the day we had a baptism service that seemed to mark a turnaround milestone for us.

Chris was being baptized, and he was a great example of how the hearts of the people began to change. Chris had attended our church for about six years but had never really engaged. His wife, Danielle, served on the worship team, which Chris resisted, and he always sat in the back.

He had told me his story, how he had been raised in a toxic church environment with a legalistic faith he just couldn't stomach. He had married Danielle, who had come to Christ through a recovery ministry in Minnesota. Her faith was critical to her survival, so being in church was not optional for her. The two of them were certainly not on the same page spiritually.

Then Chris came to a point of crisis, and he broke down emotionally in the parking lot of his work. He called his father, who talked with him over the next two hours, and Chris came to Jesus. Nearly everyone in the church knew his story, so on the Sunday he was baptized after sharing what had happened, the place erupted.

When he came out of the water, there was a standing ovation with clapping, whistling, and cheering for what Jesus was doing in Chris and in us as a church. For the first time in years, baptisms became a regular part of our schedule, as God brought more and more wandering children back to His heart through our church. It was an amazing season to witness.

Meanwhile, we were stuck financially, and still making huge payments each month on a campus we couldn't use. We had been waiting for nearly three years to get paid our $5 million for the sale of our campus. We were hanging by a thread.

It was now 2008. George W. Bush was president, and we were about to be hit by the worst recession since the Great Depression. Just as God was changing our hearts and things were looking up relationally, we were about to take another financial nosedive. What a ride.

◄ 7 ►
NICKELS AND NOSES

DEALING WITH THE FINANCES OF A TURNAROUND CHURCH is like balancing an elephant on a tightrope. The rope has to be stronger than normal, and the elephant doesn't want to be there—and if you're honest with yourself, neither do you.

Like most churches, we faced constant financial shortages. But a turnaround church is a financially unique situation: Each turnaround church has a huge capacity for institutional memory; the church members clearly remember when the church had more money than it has now. That was our situation.

Before 2005, I would often hear thinly veiled complaints like, "We used to have more money for kids' ministry," or, "We used to be able to sponsor students for camp," or, "Why can't we upgrade our phone system? We never used to have a problem staying current with equipment."

To each of these I wanted to say, "Yes, and we used to be a church of 2000 people, and now we're 250." But I never used that line. Such a response would have served no purpose, and it would have put me in more hot water.

Our financial situation remained precarious. We were making $22,000 in monthly interest payments to Church Development Fund (CDF). Our entire monthly income from giving at this point was about $38,000 per month, so you can see that we certainly couldn't make these payments out of our general fund.

At the same time, International Full Gospel Fellowship (IFGF) couldn't get their loan, so it looked like we would have to wait indefinitely for our payoff while they made monthly payments. That brought construction on our new campus to a halt. For usable meeting space, we were now renting back from IFGF part of the campus we used to own. IFGF was meeting in the sanctuary, and we were meeting in the gym on campus, setting up every week just like a church plant.

We basically owned part of two campuses, but we couldn't fully use either one. It was very frustrating for me personally, but I tried to keep a good face. Since IFGF owed us about $5 million and we owed CDF $5 million, our monthly interest payments were about the same. As long as they paid us, we could pay. If this money merry-go-round ever stopped, everything would come crashing down. So IFGF made their $22,000 monthly interest payments to us, and we paid our $22,000 monthly interest payments to CDF.

IFGF was also paying CDF an additional payment on the $2 million borrowed from them. It was a financial circus that we thought would only last about six months, but it would in fact continue like this for years. Yes, years! I felt like we were hanging by a financial thread.

It was still 2008, and we were still in the worst recession since the Great Depression. I knew that Jesus was doing something powerful in our church, but I wasn't totally sure what it was. We seemed to be stuck because of finances. We couldn't finish the building we'd bought and couldn't get the money out of the one we'd sold.

It was about this time that we were running short of building funds for the first phase. We thought the $800,000 we had set aside from the sale would at least complete the first of two phases, but we were $150,000 short. I had also hoped that the sale of the property would give us enough money so we would not have to endure a capital fundraising campaign. Not so.

We would end up doing three capital fundraising campaigns in two years, but this one was the most difficult. It was during Christmas, and we needed to have the money in 30 days. I didn't use any of the fundraising procedures I had in the past. There were no dinners. No letters. No personal contacts to high-capacity givers. I just got up and said, "We need $170,000 by the end of the month. All I'm asking you to do is pray and ask God what He wants you to do."

I set the date for the offering, and we did what we could. I took Brenda out for dinner to talk about what we could give. We had a fishing boat that I dearly loved, but we sold it and gave the largest offering we've ever given.

I wasn't the only one. Many people sacrificed. One man sold his house to avoid foreclosure, but he gave all his furniture to Creekside Church, which we in turn sold. Someone else had received an inheritance during that time and gave substantially. Another older woman had been saving in secret for a vacation with her whole family, and she gave all of it. When the offering was totaled, we had received just over $173,000. I was shocked.

I got up to announce the results on that Sunday, but I did so with a heavy heart. On the Saturday night before, a trusted staff member, Dan Metteer, let me know he was leaving us. Dan was deeply loved by our church and had worked faithfully with me for six years and was now moving on. I wished him the best, but my emotions were conflicted as I announced this great offering, knowing next Sunday I'd be announcing Dan's leaving.

Pastoral ministry is often like this. A blessing comes on the heels of a disaster, and a loss on the heels of a gain. But we move forward nonetheless.

God blessed us tremendously through that offering, but the church's weekly giving was always a struggle. This was the season when regular paychecks became a thing of the past. As I said, I got paid, just rarely on time. It was not unusual to wait a week or two before cashing a paycheck, and once I waited two months. I also took a $10,000 a year cut in pay which lasted for three years. I could not have made it without a side business that we had in our home. But I was not the only one struggling.

After Dan's leaving, the only full-time pastoral staff member we had was Jason Deuman. Jason is very loyal and the longest-serving staff member I've ever had—not to mention he's my son-in-law. Jason had always told my daughter, Kathy, before they got married that he never wanted to work for her father. She said that was fine, because she didn't want to marry a pastor. They both lost out.

I had to call in Jason and tell him that I had some bad news. He was going to have to take a huge cut in pay as well. I didn't know how long he would have to endure this, but I asked him if he were still willing to walk this journey with me. He said yes. Within a week or two, he found a part-time job and was now bi-vocational. It's not as cool as it sounds.

About this time, Kathy was about to give birth to their first child, and there were complications with the pregnancy. I watched Jason stand in faith for their finances and the health of their family. It was a tense time for all of us.

It is one thing to be a lead pastor and have faith for the situation God has called you to walk through, but it is something else entirely to watch someone else have faith because of your decisions. Jason was being loyal to me, but at a much deeper level, he was being loyal to Jesus. Watching him inspired me.

It was a good thing to have family around me during this time. In addition to the support from my wife, Brenda, I had Jason's support on staff, and my father was still working with the seniors. I know too much family can be a bad thing, but in stressful seasons, it was comforting that I really could count on family.

In August, the purchasing contract was up with IFGF. Their balloon payment was due, but they had no money to pay us. So we agreed that we would use the gym, which they owned and we had been renting, for free. But September came and went, and then October, with no payment.

I knew we were fighting a spiritual war for the soul of Creekside Church, though the finances were a very tangible battle. I knew the enemy did not want us to win. I also knew we would win. I just didn't know how. This situation was so far beyond the scope of what I'd imagined could happen that I knew Jesus had to be involved somehow.

I remember talking with Pastor Chris on the phone at one point, again conflicted emotionally. On one hand, Chris was my brother in Christ, and I wanted to stand with him in faith. On the other hand, he owed us money. It wasn't that he *wouldn't* pay, it was that he *couldn't* pay. Then, almost overnight, it turned.

You may recall that in October of 2008 President Bush signed into law the "Troubled Asset Relief Program" (TARP) of $700 billion dollars. I never dreamed that such a decision would affect our situation, but it did.

IFGF had sold a portion of their campus to a Jewish school, but the school still owed $1 million dollars. The Jewish school had completed a loan application with Bank of America, who had a reputation for working with nonprofit organizations, but they had been denied due to the economy. IFGF owed Creekside Church $5 million dollars and had also completed a loan application with Bank of America, but they had also been denied. Both applications remained on file with Bank of America.

In October of 2008, when the $700 billion in TARP funds were released, Bank of America received $45 billion. Now they had money to lend, but they decided not to receive any new nonprofit applications. Instead, they would process the applications on file.

Since IFGF and the Jewish school both had applications on file, each received a loan in short order. The Jewish school paid IFGF the $1 million they owed them. This improved IFGF's financial picture, so their $5 million loan was approved. Within two weeks the entire amount was paid off, and we were back to work on our new campus. In contrast to the earlier phases of this deal, this final phase happened quite fast. We had been slugging it out financially from November 2004 to October of 2008. Now it looked like we had some light at the end of a very long tunnel.

I'd like to say that was the end of our financial challenges, but as you already know, that's not the case. It seems that God loves to use financial pressure to change us both personally and as a church. I've learned that God uses building programs to change people and churches.

Now we launched into completing our new campus with a fury, but I was concerned about our cash flow once we moved in. What would it take for us to live in these new digs? We had done our due diligence to estimate costs, but we'd been renters for nearly five years. What kind of a shift were we in for?

Once we received our payoff from IFGF, we paid off most of the loan to CDF, and they generously said they would carry the contract on the remaining $1 million needed to finish up the campus. We estimated what it would cost to complete our remodel and set the move-in date for Easter Sunday 2009.

Finally, the day came for us to move into our new campus. It was completed, and we rejoiced. At our last Sunday in the gym, we planned to walk the distance to our new campus, about seven miles. About 100 people, all wearing Creekside Church T-shirts, walked the distance. Two sister churches, Shoreline Community Church and Westminster

Community Church each came out to supply water, and their congregations cheered us on as we walked by.

The next Sunday, April 9, 2009, was our first Sunday in our new building. It was packed. We swelled to 408 people. Every chair was taken, and people were lined up around the walls. The energy was incredible! We felt like we were on a roll.

But the next week we were down to under 200 again. Every pastor knows what the Sunday after Christmas or Easter is like. It's usually a letdown, and this was no different.

I still had this knot in my stomach about our church's finances. Would we grow enough to pay for this place and do what Jesus wanted us to do? My wife, Brenda, has reminded me of a business meeting we had just before we moved into our new campus, when I challenged the people with these words: "We have enough money to get into the building, but not enough to stay there if we don't grow. Your prayers and the people you bring will make this a success."

I began to talk with other pastors about some kind of a reserve fund and how much we might need, because I knew we'd need a reserve until we started to grow. It is crazy now to think about what we tried to do as a church of 175 people, but it happened. One pastor said his church grew enough that they made budget in six months after moving into their new building, but another pastor said he waited five years to get to the break-even point. We didn't have five years. At best we could survive about eighteen months. We were like a big Boeing 747 flying around; if we didn't find a tanker up here somewhere, we were going to fall out of the sky.

Then the tanker showed up. No, it wasn't somebody's rich uncle. It was another pastor who served as a coach to me. His work has changed our church dramatically. He challenged me to see giving in a whole new way, and as a result our church's general fund giving has increased on average 15–18 percent a year for the last four years.

I met Nelson Searcy through a mutual friend, Brandon Beals. Brandon pastors in Everett, Washington, just north of us. He is an amazing young leader and a successful church planter. I have immense respect for him.

Brandon and I met one day, and I said, "Brandon, I'm desperate. We're about to move into our new campus, and the monthly payments, utilities, and operational expenses are going to put some real pressure on us. I'm hearing that you guys are weathering this recession in great shape. What is your secret?"

Brandon said, "I'm in a coaching network with Nelson Searcy each month. I'm learning some great stuff, and some of the most amazing things have to do with money."

"Like what?" I said, eager to get something hopeful in my ears.

"Well," Brandon began, "Nelson said that you should get to a place where 50 percent of your weekly offerings come from outside the Sunday giving."

I reacted, "You're kidding! How is that ever going to happen?"

"Well, think about this," Brandon said. "Not everyone comes to your church each week. And in most churches, if they don't come, they don't give, right?"

"Of course," I said, starting to understand where he was going.

Brandon then said, "If only 40 or 50 percent of your church is in service each week, you can increase your giving just by giving options. Nelson's church, Journey, has 85 percent of the giving coming in from outside the Sunday offering.

"Giving happens in several ways, not just through the Sunday offering. It can happen through online giving, auto-debit, or business-reply envelopes in the program. There is also clear follow-up on each new giver and a broader understanding of each stage a new giver goes through as they grow spiritually. The bottom line is that stewardship is part of discipleship."

Brandon went on to explain how this would work, and I was intrigued, not just with the stewardship strategy but with the coaching as well. I asked him if he could get me into the coaching network. He said he'd try, and he did.

For the next year, Brandon and I traveled to New York each month to receive coaching from Nelson Searcy. We would leave Seattle on a Thursday morning, fly six hours, grab dinner, and get to our hotel. We went through coaching on Friday and flew home after class. It was a 36-hour turnaround, but well worth the investment. This information was strategic in nature and provided a path for moving forward in eight basic systems.

Over the next three years, we applied this biblical coaching to our church and saw dramatic results. As of this writing, we have seen a 15–18 percent increase in giving each year, during a recession. We recently reached the point where, indeed, 50 percent of our giving—and sometimes more—comes in from outside the Sunday offering.

I eventually went on to complete two years of coaching with Nelson Searcy and became a certified coach myself. For information on each of those systems check out www.churchleaderinsights.com.

Giving is the fuel of ministry in many ways. There is so much we could do and would do if we only had the money. We believe that God has the money and power, but we don't connect the dots: God keeps His money in our bank accounts.

Giving is always a matter of the heart. Jesus said:

> *Do not store up for yourselves treasures on earth, where moths and vermin destroy, and where thieves break in and steal. But store up for yourselves treasures in heaven, where moths and vermin do not destroy, and where thieves do not break in and steal. For where your treasure is, there your heart will be also. Matthew 6:19–21*

Jesus said, "Show me your money, and I'll show you your heart." Our giving and our heart have always been connected. And we serve a generous God, who generously sent His Son to save us. He wants us to learn to be generous too.

So as a part of applying Nelson's coaching, and following God's model of generosity, we started receiving a Christmas offering, asking the people to give generously. We launched the idea of a Christmas offering in 2010, with a goal of $10,000. The most we'd ever given during Christmas up to this point was $2,500. Targeting four times that amount was a challenge.

It was one thing to raise money for a building program, because that would be money we'd use at home, but a Christmas offering was going to be totally given away. This was the first of several lessons God was teaching us on how to be generous as a church.

We were changing and growing spiritually and numerically as a church. The poverty mentality that we had been living in was leaving, and we were learning to trust God and be obedient. When we received our Christmas Eve offering that year, it was over $12,000.

So the next year, 2011, we challenged the people to give $15,000. They gave $18,000. In 2012 we challenged the people to give $25,000, and they gave $32,000. And in 2012 we challenged them to give $50,000, and they gave $94,000. Wow!

Now I need to say at this point that we began to focus more clearly on where the money would be used and how it would be divided. We put 50 percent of the Christmas offering toward "Creekside Global," our missions program, and 50 percent toward "Creekside Local," which meant relaunching Creekside to better serve our community.

The generosity of Creekside Church began to grow in other areas as well. We decided to pay the overhead for our café out of the general fund and give all of the money made on Sundays to World Vision's Clean Water Fund, to help build wells in developing nations. On average, our Clean Water Café currently provides a new well about every ten months.

Sometimes, being generous takes on a practical, tangible look. During one summer Sunday, my oldest daughter, Kelly felt like Jesus wanted us to take our shoes off and give them to those without shoes. She was nervous as she shared with the church, but dozens of people lined up their shoes, some brand-new, across the stage. Later, they were collected and given to the Union Gospel Mission, a local shelter.

Jesus also asked us to be generous to single moms. Our "Single Mom Sunday" in October 2012 turned out to be the highest-attended day we've ever had since our turnaround began. We asked everyone to bring their single-mom friends to church so that we could give them a gift and have the elders pray for them.

Each of the 31 single moms who showed up received a gift envelope and a blessing. Many opened their card right there and were shocked to receive a crisp $100 bill. We had nearly 650 people that day. It was electric.

We repeated this blessing again seven months later on Mother's Day. Only this time Jesus told us to bless those outside our church. We asked people to give us the names and addresses of single moms they knew. We also had adopted a local elementary school and arranged to deliver gifts to the single moms with children in their school as well.

Then we linked up with a dozen local businesses and created coupons to give out to single moms on Mother's Day, providing money to spend as well. Some coupons were practical—haircuts and groceries—others were designed to make mom and her kids feel special—restaurants, ice cream, and pedicures. It was an opportunity for us as a church to bless our community. Altogether, we reached out to 131 single moms with cash and coupons, and only a quarter of those were part of Creekside Church.

This outreach cost us the equivalent of one Sunday morning offering, about $15,000, and we could never have helped these mothers if we didn't have the resources. We could never have been generous to others if we hadn't learned that our generous God wanted us to learn to be generous like Him. God used the stewardship system and the Christmas offering strategy from Nelson Searcy as a key part of being able to bless our community.

During this period of time, we began to grow again. In October of 2009, after being in our new campus for only seven months, we launched a second service. We now had services at 9 AM and 11 AM. It was a stretch, especially for children's ministry and volunteers, but I knew that if we didn't add services, we could not grow.

We grew by 22 percent in 2009 to an average Sunday morning attendance of just under 300 people. We stayed with that two-service schedule for the next year and then added a 6 PM service in February of 2011. I have to say that the 6 PM service did not take off like the morning services. But we kept at it, and it finally gained traction.

My friend Charles Arn, in his book, How to Start a New Service, says that often a new service will take a year or so to gain consistency. I found that to be true for sure. As a pastor, I thought a new service should take off in a few months. But if people came three out of four Sundays, which hardly ever happened, and they attended this new service for a year, that meant they had been there only forty hours. That is the equivalent to one full week of work.

A growing church will offer more services to give people more options. People get to choose when they worship, and sometimes even where and how they worship, as churches offer different venues and service styles. This obviously requires great flexibility on the part of the leadership and culture of the church, but growing things are flexible.

This is another reason why every turnaround church must have a significant shift in culture. Otherwise, the flexibility needed to adjust in finances and in a service schedule can't happen. New services are one of the best ways to reach your community and see your church grow.

Going from one service to two is the hardest jump to make. When I coach pastors, I encourage them to never say "two services" because that is limited. If you add a service, you are now a "multiple-service church," not a "two-service church." It is significantly easier to go from two services to three or four services than from one service to two services.

As of this writing, we are launching a five-service schedule for the fall of 2013. We are adding a hymn-based service called "Softer Sunday" and a Spanish service to better reach our community. So we will look like this:

9:00 AM	Softer Sunday in fellowship hall
9:30 AM	Contemporary service in main auditorium
11:15 AM	Contemporary service in main auditorium
1:00 PM	Spanish service in fellowship hall
6:00 PM	Contemporary service in main auditorium

As you can see, having a service in a different location on campus allows us to overlap the services. That way, whoever is teaching will be able to shuttle from one auditorium to another. Also, I will not be doing all of the teaching in these services. Developing a teaching team is key to making multiple services work effectively and to creating sustainability. I will write more on the teaching-team strategy later.

Since launching a multiple-service format, we have experienced a 22 percent growth rate each year for the last three years. Well over 65 percent of the people at Creekside Church have joined during that timeframe.

We are now getting ready to launch new campuses, but I will also write more on that later. First, we need to understand what makes a turnaround pastor tick.

INSIGHT FROM LEADERS

Last fall, our church stepped out in faith and made the investment to join the Turnaround Church Coaching Network with Don Ross. From the first monthly session we realized we couldn't afford not to be involved in this coaching opportunity. What we learned helped us overcome significant limitations and gave us solid solutions to the leadership blind spots and ministry opportunities that we were simply missing.

I can't think of anything in the last 28 years of ministry that has so transformed my philosophy and helped me clearly define my theology of ministry. This coaching network is really a discipleship strategy for pastors and staff. It's one thing to know what you are called to and what you want to see, yet quite another when you break down the needed steps to getting there.

In our implementation of what we learned caused us to rethink much of what we considered about leadership and church. Immediately we saw fruit in our finances, people's commitment to areas of ministry, leadership development, and growth. During the coaching duration we went to multiple services and developed numerous ministries. We have had an impact in our volunteers, excellence in our Weekend Worship Services, and stability in our follow-up, outreach and assimilation.

Turnaround Church Coaching Network forced me to ask better questions in every area of myself as a person and the church God has called me to serve. We have seen incredible fruit in every area we have tackled. The considerable growth we have experienced so outweighs the original investment we made. This opportunity has changed our leadership and our Church. I recommend this opportunity to any church no matter the size to make this investment as we move ahead in excellence in His Kingdom.

Pastor Eric Roberts
New Life Assembly
Bremerton, WA

◄ 8 ►
TURNAROUND PASTOR PROFILE

LEADING A TURNAROUND CHURCH is more art than science for sure, and becoming a turnaround pastor takes more than desire. With 80 percent of the churches in the United States plateaued or declining, we need more leaders to step up.

I have said in my turnaround-coaching network that churches don't get stuck—pastors get stuck; and that is both true and untrue. It is untrue if you have inherited a plateaued or declining church as the new pastor, but you will be challenged soon enough with your set of courageous decisions. Don't be afraid, though, you have a Great Advocate who will see you through.

On the other hand, the statement is true because churches follow leaders. If you are leading a church that was once growing and is now in decline, or one that has never grown, you may be stuck. A church is considered to be in decline if it has lost 10 percent or more in average Sunday attendance in the last five years. I knew our church was declining. I successfully led our church from 600 to 175 in nine years. It was incredibly hard to stay with the church; but honestly, I needed a job, and no one else was calling. Plus, Jesus said, "Stick with it; better days are coming." I love the way He consistently gave me hope.

If you are leading a declining church, I can sympathize with you, but we both know sympathy won't change the course of your church. Decisions do that. And if you know the decisions you need to make, and you can't or won't make them, then stuck is the right word. Again, I can fully appreciate the pain of such decisions. I have lived through this turnaround process.

Consider this: if Jesus put you in your church, then He must think you have what it takes to lead it. Jesus believes in you. At this point that needs to be enough.

I remember when I concluded that Jesus had called me to this task of leading our turnaround. And if He had called me, there must be no one better for this job. If there were, He would have called him or her. It was at that point that my confidence and skill set began to grow.

My wife and I had many conversations about our church during the hard years. We both agreed that what we were doing wasn't worth the money, but it was worth the sacrifice to move Christ's kingdom forward. So I learned to change and become who He needed me to be, to lead this church to become what it needed to be. I learned to be more decisive, not to be sidetracked by the inevitable criticism and to keep our church focused on the mission.

Turnaround churches have experienced a decline nearly impossible to reverse, but somehow they do reverse it. Most churches in similar situations simply go out of business. What are the critical aspects of a church and pastor that see terminal decline turned into growth?

Let's begin by defining a turnaround church. A turnaround church has recognized that, due to consistent decline, it will soon be out of business, but the leader and this church have courageously decided to face the truth and make a series of extremely difficult and painful decisions to reverse that trend.

So what is that skill set? What does the profile of a turnaround pastor look like? Here are twelve criteria for you to consider. I hope you'll use them as a personal checklist.

MISSION

I'd like to say, "Everything rises or falls on mission,", but I think John Maxwell has already captured that sentiment. Regardless, mission is critical. Understanding that both the leader and the church are part of Christ's mission to reach lost people will develop the needed character qualities and leadership skills to embrace a turnaround and survive the initial pain that will come.

Mission says, "This is not about me; it's about Jesus." When we understand that nearly 4,000 churches go out of business each year and we are not planting nearly enough to replace them, we can understand that turning around declining churches is very much a part of Christ's mission.

As I said in chapter 1, the challenge of a turnaround church was written for us 2,000 years ago in Revelation. Jesus speaks to the church of Sardis:

You have a reputation of being alive, but you are dead. Wake up! Strengthen what remains and is about to die...
Revelation 3:2

In a very real sense, a declining church may have had a reputation of being alive, but it is not alive now. It's on life support and needs help. Both the pastor and church leaders need to work together to "strengthen what remains and is about to die." This is hard work but possible, if the leaders and church are willing to do what is needed not only to survive but to thrive.

Often, though, the pastor is viewed as a threat because the church has no mission other than survival. The new pastor shows up, or a rejuvenated pastor tries to cast vision for a better day, and the change is resisted. The resistance happens because moving the mission forward requires risk, and a church based on pure survival can't and won't risk. If you lead, or try to force, the church in that direction, it can become a war zone.

Each decision can become a tug-of-war between the pastor and board, and Christ is not served by such tension. This is often the case if the pastor has been brought in to rescue the church through his leadership. The church sees the pastor as the answer person—until the pastor makes a decision that upsets the church culture.

But regardless of the situation, mission is critical. I believe having a mission statement that reflects the core of the church's heartbeat is also critical. I have never seen a church reverse their decline without a clear and compelling mission.

A helpful book on understanding and developing a mission in your church is Aubrey Malphurs' Advanced Strategic Planning. It helped me see the possibility of a new day and gave me a plan to move forward.

MISSION REFLECTION QUESTIONS

1. Do you have a compelling mission in the church you lead?

2. Do you have a mission statement that reflects it?

3. Does your church understand, believe, and emotionally embrace this mission?

4. Do you use your mission statement as both a compass for direction and a filter to know what to say yes and no to?

VISION

A turnaround church is usually led by a visionary leader, often one brought in from outside the church so the leader is not a part of the current culture. The value of bringing in a new leader is that they are not stuck in the current thought trends or bogged down by the church's history. The challenge of a new visionary leader is that they must earn the right to lead a group of people, almost all of whom are stuck in current thought trends and severely bogged by down the church's history.

There is great debate about having a mission statement and a vision statement and a purpose statement and strategy statement and a bank statement and a... Well, you get the picture. I've worked with churches that had precise statements for mission, vision, and purpose but were still hopelessly stuck. They thought if they had good statements, it would move them forward. But written statements do not lead a church out of decline. Leaders do!

Instead of multiple statements, we decided to have one clear mission statement that people could buy into. It has vision and purpose too, but we only preach one statement. We have that one statement on our program, the side of the church, the interior wall, and the media screen. If I could, I'd have it tattooed on new members. (Not really. Well, maybe...)

Our mission statement reflects our vision, because if we live up to our mission, then we will be a very different church in five years. You can't have a mission statement without vision, and people sense that. So why confuse them with a bunch of different statements? I will write more on this later as we walk through the turnaround strategy.

Andy Stanley's book *Visioneering* was extremely helpful and practical in understanding how to cast vision and make it stick.

VISION REFLECTION QUESTIONS

1. Do you have a clear picture in your mind of your church's pre-ferred future? If yes, could you list some of the critical features of that vision?

2. As you look at the list of vision-based elements you've written, how would your current leadership community support them?

3. Take a few moments and write down at least ten ways you can communicate various aspects of the vision with your church.

LEADERSHIP

This pastor/leader must be able to paint a constant verbal picture of a church's preferred future, based in reality. He must also realize, regardless of what those around him say, that he is probably the only one who sees it, and often it will be foggy even to him. Nevertheless, there is a God-given picture, and he must hold on to it relentlessly.

Author Max De Pree said, "The first responsibility of a leader is to define reality. The last is to say thank you. In between, the leader is a servant." The pastor of a turnaround church must develop the skill set necessary to tell the truth without discouraging their flock beyond recovery. The ability to chart a manageable course, encourage people, and recognize the smallest progress is critical.

Learning to be a leader means making decisions. There is no escaping it. Show me a leader who is not leading by making clear, understandable decisions, and I'll show you a church that is stuck. Often I knew which decision needed to be made, but the emotional price tag was so great that I refused to make it. I postponed critical decisions out of fear, but Jesus was gracious and would eventually bring me back around so I could have another chance to make the same decision I should have made earlier.

LEADERSHIP REFLECTIONS QUESTIONS

1. What situation in your church or life requires you to make a courageous decision?

2. How long have you known about it?

3. What has prevented you from making a decision before now?

4. If you continue to postpone leading and making this decision, what will be the eventual outcome?

5. What does Jesus want you to do?

PAIN

Another element needed is the ability to endure pain. This is directly connected to leadership because painful decisions will be required for you to lead a turnaround church. There is no such thing as pain-free ministry. Jesus led through pain, Paul led through pain, and so will you if you are called to lead. Often this pain will be the emotional pain of rejection, but financial pain and even physical pain may be a part of the process. The old saying, "No pain, no gain," could not be more applicable.

Let's be painfully honest here. If the current way of doing things at your church were working, it wouldn't need to turn around. People have taken ownership of the things that are being done. So in order to change the way things are done, the people must change. Either they must change internally or their position must be changed to allow new people to do what they used to. This change can be incredibly painful for both pastor and people, but it does move the mission forward.

Imagine telling someone who is very faithful that they need to change their way of leading a class or ministry, even though they have done it this way for years or even decades. They can feel driven away by the pastor if the mission has not been successfully and clearly communicated. Even then, emotions usually overrule any sense of commitment to the mission.

I learned a strategy for dealing with some pain. As I mentioned in chapter 3, I learned to wait three days before making a difficult decision. Similarly, after receiving a nasty email or phone call, I would give myself permission not to respond for three days. It was remarkable how, during that time, the emotions settled and perspective returned. Now a three-day break from responding didn't mean the person who hurt me was more pleasant or the situation was safe, but having perspective helped me deal with the emotional pressure. I wasn't able to give myself three days in every situation, but often I could. When I applied this principle, it really helped give me endurance.

PAIN REFLECTION QUESTIONS

1. Where do you feel pain in your life and/or ministry?

2. Do you know the source of this pain? Is the source a person or a situation?

3. How have you been hurt personally by this situation or person?

4. Have you been able to forgive and move on?

5. What steps do you need to take to do that?

ENDURANCE

Although things must change, it will take time. Researcher Gary McIntosh states that a turnaround can take from five to twelve years, depending on the setting. Rural churches and churches in dire circumstances can take longer. (Ours was a dire-circumstance church, and we took a bit longer.) The more desperate the situation, the more endurance is needed on the part of the leader.

> *For this very reason, make every effort to add to your faith goodness; and to goodness, knowledge; and to knowledge, self-control; and to self-control, perseverance; and to perseverance, godliness; and to godliness, mutual affection; and to mutual affection, love. For if you possess these qualities in increasing measure, they will keep you from being ineffective and unproductive in your knowledge of our Lord Jesus Christ. II Peter 1:5–8*

It is interesting that perseverance is listed right between self-control and Godliness. You can't have perseverance without self-control, and you're not Godly without perseverance. No one has more perseverance than God, so learning to persevere and endure is part of growing spiritually as well as growing as a leader.

More than once I was called a bulldog because I wouldn't let go. My endurance would ebb and flow, and I would get tired from lack of success and forward motion. But Jesus sustained me. There were many times when I wanted to quit, but I didn't want to look at Christ one day and tell Him, "It was just too hard. You should have sent someone else."

I made some changes to the way I worked to add to my endurance. I became an early riser, usually around 5 AM, and then I went home in the early afternoon. I took up fishing and did regular mission trips. This allowed me to rest and be out of the environment of stress.

ENDURANCE REFLECTION QUESTIONS

1. On a scale of 1–10, with 1 being *worn out* and 10 being *full of endurance*, where would you place yourself now?

2. What are the top three things that steal your ability to endure and persevere?

3. What changes can you make to remove some of the stress you deal with and add to your endurance?

4. What meaningful recreation do you practice?

MONEY MANAGEMENT

I've already written a chapter on this, but here are some more thoughts because this is a critical skill. If you can handle money well, people will trust you. If you mess up with money, it will be a problem. And it will be a big problem if you try to hide it.

Here's the deal in turnaround churches: money will be tight. Period. A new vision will draw in resources. But it takes a while to see a new vision surface. That's the downside.

The upside is that declining churches often have untapped resources in facilities and property. These can be tapped to pick up the needed capital to make changes and simply stay alive. We tapped our equity several times to make changes and to move us ahead.

There were also times when we needed to make some changes that had no apparent impact, like a new roof or a new heating system. Those were necessary maintenance issues, but it's hard to cast vision for a new furnace. So we would add something tangible and visible to help move the mission forward, especially in the area of kids and youth. This was not done as a token gesture to get money for the real project, but it's always wise to add something visible to the unseen need. There is a reason why it's called *vision*—you have to help people see it first.

Also, the pastor should be prepared to resource himself during a turnaround recovery. By this I mean he may have to work a second job or set funds aside to "float" his finances until he gets paid. I've already addressed this, but just knowing it in advance will help you emotionally and financially.

MONEY MANAGEMENT REFLECTION QUESTIONS

1. Does your church function on a budget? If so do you have a clear process for developing it? Write out that process and then think through what needs to be changed or adjusted.

2. How do you publically show yourself to be fiscally responsible to your church? How do you produce Annual reports for your members? Do you have regular board meetings with financials being presented?

3. Does your church have any financial conflicts in its past? If so how will you or how have you dealt with them?

FACILITIES

These are important but not necessarily first in your thinking and planning. You don't have to be a building expert to lead a turnaround. Buildings are not the church, and God does not live on a church campus. Acts 7:48 says, "The Most High does not live in houses made by human hands."

When we moved into our new campus, we purposely did not create a sanctuary; we have a "Big Room." We did not want our church to have such a focus on buildings that we could think the church did its work on the campus. I'm not saying the word *sanctuary* is wrong. I'm saying it is easy for us to think, act, and live like the church is a building—but it isn't a building. Conversely, it is usually exceptionally hard for a turnaround church to think, act, and live like the church is not a building. Most churches have sacrificed to keep their facilities in great shape, and therein lies the problem.

Usually an established congregation is deeply rooted to facilities, having sacrificed to build and maintain them. This means it is easy to actually have the building become an idol. If it becomes necessary to sell, adjust, or even just go outside of the building to move the mission forward, and your church is unwilling to do that, you may have an idol on your hands.

Most turnaround churches will make some kind of adjustments to their facilities at some point. Any changes you make should be done carefully, as part of an overall plan. Getting key lay leaders on board is critical.

Remember, buildings are not the church; they are a tool. Sometimes you need to sharpen or replace tools to accomplish a worthy project. We did. As a part of our turnaround, we relocated and sold our old campus. I'm not saying that is a good strategy for all churches, but we knew we needed a drastic change and I knew God was leading this direction.

FACILITY REFLECTION QUESTIONS

1. Do your facilities enhance your church's mission or impede it? Explain.

2. What would you change about your facilities, and what do you think that change would produce for you?

3. Have you talked with key leaders about this change? If so, is there excitement or resistance?

4. If there is resistance, is the idea being resisted, or is something else (presentation, timing, etc.)?

TENURE

One of the qualities you'll need as a turnaround pastor is tenure. You will need to simply plan to be there a long time before you gain the influence needed to make key decisions. There is no shortcut. I wish there were, but there isn't.

Researcher George Barna says in his book *Turnaround Churches* that most turnaround pastors will lead only one turnaround church in their career. I think that's probably true, not only because of stress and the energy it takes but also the amount of time it takes. If you are unwilling to give five years to see a declining church turn around, don't get involved. The whole project will take more time than five years, but you will see progress by then.

Trust is the most crucial, intangible quality a pastor needs to turn a declining church, and it takes a while to gain that trust. You will, quite literally, be asked to lay down your life for this church, one day at a time.

I remember that for years I did only a few of the weddings, funerals, and baby dedications in our church. Those are key milestones where a pastor will bond with a family. Often a former pastor would be invited to officiate at those events. It was a little frustrating, but I understood that each family wanted a trusted leader, whom they knew and loved, to be with them.

When you think about it, it really doesn't matter how long it takes to turn a church around, does it? Do you have something better to do? If Jesus has asked you to lead a turnaround in this church, and you said yes, then relax. Jesus already knows how long it's going to take. Enjoy the ride. Let your tenure and influence build as you love the people and obey the Lord.

Being a turnaround leader is rewarding, but much like parents who wait years before being appreciated by their children, you will need to be willing to wait and endure to see the results you are working toward. There is no quick fix to reverse direction in a declining church. But it can happen, and it needs to happen.

TENURE REFLECTION QUESTIONS

1. How long are you willing to give to the church you serve? Will you give three years, five years, ten years or more?

2. Do you feel anxious about the progress you've made and wish things would move faster? How do you think the people you serve interpret that anxiety?

3. Would you be willing to serve this church the rest of your life, if Jesus asked you to? Why or why not?

PEER SUPPORT

Lone rangers make poor turnaround church pastors. It is just too challenging to do this project alone. You will need to build around you a group of other leaders from outside your church. They'll need to believe in you and what you are doing, and you'll need to trust them deeply.

These leaders will listen to you as you process your plans, reflect back to you pressure points, and talk you through the minefield in which you work. You will need them, and God will give them to you. Don't do this alone.

I have a group that I meet with each Thursday morning. It started with just four of us, but it has grown to about 15 now. Not everyone comes every week, and there is no agenda. I send out a reminder, and whoever can come is welcome. We pray for each other, trade sermons and ideas, and give unbelievable amounts of support.

After I crashed in the ministry in 1993, I made up my mind that I would never be without critical support again, so I asked a few guys to join me for breakfast. That is how it started. Sometimes the guys and I have shared deep heart concerns for our churches, families, and situations. Other times we've laughed and cut up the whole time, making preacher jokes no one else would get or think funny.

Here's what I know: any one of those brothers would stand up with me anytime I need them, and I'd do the same for them. We are a band of brothers, and we stand together.

Any pastor can have this; you just have to ask someone to join you. Don't sit around waiting to be invited. It will never happen. Put a list of guys together, and ask them to start meeting with you regularly. Over time, you will grow to love, support, and help each other in amazing ways.

PEER SUPPORT REFLECTION QUESTIONS

1. Do you have trusted pastor friends that you meet with regularly, or do you feel like a Lone Ranger?

2. Do they have permission to ask you the hard questions? Do you have permission to ask them the hard questions?

3. How have they helped you process a difficult church situation?

4. How do you support one another (with resources, ideas, time away, etc.)?

GOD'S WORD

You must have a high view of Scripture to be an effective turnaround pastor. Being able to "download" encouragement from God's Word, where you know He is talking to you, is an important skill. Remember, Jesus is the one in Revelation who said, "Strengthen what remains," which is exactly what you are attempting to do. Letting Him encourage you through His Word and give you direction is very important.

Reading the biblical accounts of other turnaround leaders like Nehemiah, Joshua, and Moses is not only inspiring; it's life to you as a leader. You need a high view of Scripture.

Jesus Himself quoted Scripture when He said, "Man does not live by bread alone, but by every word that comes from God" (Matthew 4:4). The turnaround pastor for sure needs more than bread. We need to have God talk to us often through His Word.

GOD'S WORD REFLECTION QUESTIONS

1. Do you regularly feed on God's Word, or do you only read the Bible as a part of studying for your sermon each week?

2. If it is true that we reproduce after our own kind, then your church will feed on God's Word as you do. How does that make you feel?

3. What promises has God given you from His Word regarding your current church that you can hold onto?

SPIRIT

There must be a sense in you, your family, and your leadership core that you are being led by the Holy Spirit in this endeavor. Leading a turnaround church is an adventure in resurrection, and the Holy Spirit is better than you at raising the dead.

Jesus called the Holy Spirit *the Advocate* (John 16:7), and anyone leading a turnaround church will need an advocate to guide him or her. The Holy Spirit will be your life coach, guiding you through tense meetings, difficult financial decisions, and developing a critical strategy to save this church. He wants this church to move forward with Christ's mission more than you do, and He knows how to get it done.

I learned during this time to fellowship with the Holy Spirit in prayer. Paul said, "May the grace of the Lord Jesus Christ, and the love of God, and the fellowship of the Holy Spirit be with you all" (II Cor. 13:14). To *fellowship* means to spend time together, to confide and talk and listen. Many of the ideas that moved us forward came during times alone. While driving or on the water, some amazing idea would spark inside me, and I'd be off planning. Then only later would I realize that the idea was a result of my prayer and fellowship with the Spirit.

I know there is a lot of craziness done in the name of the Holy Spirit. Some of it is embarrassing, and some of it is completely offensive. Regardless, Jesus still does send us the Holy Spirit to empower us for ministry. Some overreact and ignore Him, but He is your most trusted advocate. No one wants you to succeed more than He does.

SPIRIT REFLECTION QUESTIONS

1. What role does the Holy Spirit play in your life? Your church? Your future?

2. When you have new ideas come, do you recognize that the Spirit is the giver of "every good and perfect gift" (James 1:17)?

3. How does the Holy Spirit help you in your current assignment of leading a turnaround church?

PRAYER

The final skill I want to address is prayer, and it is a discipline and a skill. Simply put, if you stop praying, you will give up. So don't stop praying.

Then Jesus told his disciples a parable to show them that they
should always pray and not give up.
Luke 18:1

I'm not sure how much we need to pray, but I mostly know when I haven't prayed enough. I do believe in prayer, and I do pray often. But I can't honestly say that I have always factored prayer into my leadership strategy. The older I have grown, the more I have come to understand how prayer helps me see what I couldn't see before.

Often when I prayed, my mind would wander. I started thinking about other things I needed to do. One day I was confiding this with an older pastor, and He said, "Did you ever think that maybe those are not distractions? That maybe they are ideas the Holy Spirit is giving you to better organize your day?"

This thought changed my thinking. Now when I pray, I sit with a notepad to take notes on what comes to mind regarding my day. It has certainly increased my productivity and made prayer more personal.

We also need to pray as a church. I recognized some people in our church were called to prayer and thoroughly enjoyed the exercise, and others needed to discipline themselves to pray. Either way, we are still commanded to pray. So as a part of recovery as a church, we developed a few prayer events and practices to build our spiritual fortitude.

One of the first things we did was a one-year strategy called "Park and Pray." When we launched this, we still had not moved into our new campus, money was tight, and we needed to break through spiritual resistance. So I asked the people to drive up to the new campus once a week, sit in their car, and pray for 15 minutes. I gave them a list of 15 things to cover in prayer, and I asked them to pray for one minute on each.

The second event we hosted was also before we moved in, and it was called "Creekside 24." This was one of the most powerful actions we took. Basically, we read God's Word as a prayer in every room on our new campus, and we read the whole Bible in 24 hours. Here is why we did it and how it worked.

Jesus said in John 15:4, "You are clean through the word I have spoken to you." Our new campus needed cleaning. Every organization that had moved onto that campus had died.

The building was originally built as an elementary school around 1965. Later, the school district sold it to a boys' detention center, and they really tore it up before going out of business. Then a medical center bought it and used it as brain trauma center. They dropped $7 million on upgrades and then went out of business. Finally, a Bible school bought it and dropped another million dollars into it before closing its doors. We bought it from their creditors. The neighbors were literally watching to see how long we would last. Some of them are in the church now, and they've told us that it was the talk of the neighborhood. You can see we needed cleansing.

So we set up a schedule based on the number of people reading and the number of rooms we had, and it worked out that everyone would read about eleven chapters of the Bible. On April 28, 2006, starting at noon, we began reading the Bible. We continued through noon on April 29. Then we had a worship time and lunch together. It was memorable for sure. In fact, as a part of our current strategy, we will do this again in July of 2013.

After we moved in and our church began to grow, we added more services and hired more staff, and I recognized that our prayer support was not adequate. I don't know how to tell you when prayer support is adequate. I just recognize when it isn't. So I developed two prayer teams.

The first was a personal prayer team. All through the New Testament, the Apostle Paul is asking for prayer, and I remember reading in Peter Wagner's prayer series that Paul knew he needed more prayer than he could pray for himself. Now I felt the same way, so I recruited about 10 people to join me in prayer each Tuesday at 6 AM. I confide in them about challenges I'm facing personally and we're facing as a church.

They pray for my coaching network, our outreach, relationship situations, the development of this book—in fact, they pray for anything and everything that puts any kind of pressure on me. They help lift the load significantly. I can't tell you how meaningful it is to hear my concerns being lifted in prayer by other brothers and sisters.

The second prayer team is led by one of our elders. We launched it on Vision Sunday 2012. Vision Sunday is an annual day we schedule to focus on our goals for the next year, and prayer was at the top off the list for 2012. At that point, we averaged around 500 people in attendance each Sunday, and I knew our prayer foundation was inadequate for what Jesus was calling us to do. If we averaged 500 on Sunday, that meant the number of people who actually called Creekside home was about 1300. (A church is about 2.5 times its average Sunday morning attendance, because not everyone comes every Sunday.)

So I stepped out and asked God for 200 people who would pray ten minutes at night and ten minutes in the morning. We called it "Praying the Ten," and it has impacted our church. Again, I set up a strategy of one minute per item through the acrostic *PRAYER TEAM* and asked the people to spend one minute on each of the following areas:

1. **Praise:** How can I praise God my Father?
   Enter his gates with thanksgiving and his courts with praise; give thanks to him and praise his name.
   Psalm 100:4

2. **Repent:** Is the Spirit convicting me of sin?
   For I know my transgressions, and my sin is always before me. Against you, you only, have I sinned and done what is evil in your sight.
   Psalm 51:3–4

3. **Ask:** What "Big Thing" am I asking for?
   Ask and it will be given to you; seek and you will find; knock and the door will be opened to you. For everyone who asks receives; the one who seeks finds; and to the one who knocks, the door will be opened.
   Matthew 7:7–8

4. **Yield:** Am I regularly obeying the Spirit?
   If you love me, keep my commands.
   John 14:15

5. **Example:** Father, make me an example others can follow.
   Follow my example, as I follow the example of Christ.
   I Corinthians 11:1

6. Relationships: How can I love others in my relationships? My marriage, children, friends, neighbors, etc.
A new command I give you: Love one another. As I have loved you, so you must love one another. By this everyone will know that you are my disciples, if you love one another. John 13:34–35

7. Three: Who are three people the Spirit is asking me to pray for and invite to Creekside Church?

_____

_____

_____

Be wise in the way you act toward outsiders; make the most of every opportunity.
Colossians 4:5

8. Eyes and Ears: Pray that each person has a soft heart so their eyes and ears are open to the gospel.
You will be ever hearing but never understanding; you will be ever seeing but never perceiving. For this people's heart has become calloused; they hardly hear with their ears, and they have closed their eyes.
Matthew 13:14–15

9. Attitude: How does my attitude need to change to be more like Jesus' attitude?
Have the same attitude as Christ Jesus.
Philippians 2:5

10. Mission: How is God asking me to move our mission forward in helping people discover, trust, and love Jesus Christ?
I will build my church, and the gates of Hades will not over-come it.
Matthew 16:18

This was simple and easy to understand, and it helped us learn to pray as a new church. In addition to the 200 praying daily, we pray over one item each week, in concert, as a church. Many of our people are new Christians, and this has helped develop the discipline of prayer in their lives. They also see themselves helping the mission as they pray. I've had many tell me that this simple prayer plan has helped them engage in meaningful prayer. That is encouraging.

I am very grateful to Mark Batterson for his book on prayer. It provides a simple and clear understanding of the power of prayer. In fact we gave a copy of his book on prayer, *The Circle Maker*, to everyone on our prayer team. It was a good investment. Prayer always reminds me that Jesus is in charge, and not me.

INSIGHT FROM LEADERS

After leading my first church for eight years, it was clear to see that something was wrong! Our attendance was flat at about 70 people each week, our finances were weak, the morale of our folks was average at best, and there was no clear focus or direction. It just seemed like we were marking time until Jesus comes back. I knew something was wrong and the people felt it too. It felt like there was something broken. Something just wasn't working right... and it was me!

God helped me come to the realization that I did not have the skill set to lead our church to where He wanted it to go. But He did not want me to leave my church either. That's when I joined the Turnaround Church Coaching Network for a nine-month adventure. After working through this amazing coaching opportunity, not only has our church become healthier, but also I have become healthier. Almost one year after the start of the TCCN, we have seen a 50% increase in our attendance and a 25% increase in our average monthly finances. We have more people serving, we are seeing more visit, and retaining more first time guests then ever. This last year we baptized more people than the previous seven combined!!

Going through this coaching has been extremely helpful to my spiritual health. Yes, it is fun watching things turnaround in our church, but what I am most thankful for is the turnaround that happened in me. I will be forever grateful for TCCN and to the other pastors in my class who walked with me.

Pastor Drew Foster
Pleasant View Church
Post Falls, ID

◄ 9 ►
LIFECYCLE REALITIES

NOW THAT YOU HAVE SOME IDEAS regarding the profile of a turnaround pastor, let's look at the profile of a turnaround church and at the lifecycle of a church. This is critical to understanding the stages you will go through as you lead your church out of the fog and into the mission Christ has assigned you.

Like every organization, a church has a lifecycle. We would like to think that our church will go on forever—and of course the Church of Jesus Christ *will* go on forever—but our local church has a lifecycle to it.

In many ways, the profile of a turnaround church is found in a study of your church's lifecycle. Looking at the critical aspects of a local church through the lifecycle lens is very helpful and can give a clearer picture of a preferred future.

There are many studies on church lifecycles. Most conclude that a church's lifecycle will run about 50 years. Some churches may go through all five stages of the lifecycle in 40 years; others, in 60 years; but 50 years is a good average. Knowing where you are on this lifecycle will help you develop a strategy for your church's future.

I have read many of these studies on lifecycle, and each one of them is based primarily on a church's age. So knowing your church's history is important. Begin by asking questions of your congregation. This is a great exercise, and it will gain you points with your people if you show interest in their church's past, which is also your church's past.

You'll find that they will secure their memories to one or two anchors. Events and milestones will be anchored to either the name of a former senior pastor or a specific building project, so when you ask questions, focus on those two connections. As you ask about these people and projects, you are sending a message that you care about this time period, even though you weren't there. This is a loving message and a good use of your time in building relationships.

One of the experts in the field of a church's lifecycle is my friend Gary McIntosh. Any book written by Gary will help you. His book *Three Generations* saved me an incredible amount of grief as we moved to a different worship style. He helped me understand clearly how culture is imprinted on us as young adults through music. Since music is the predominant element in identifying a church's culture, this connection was critical.

Another key work by Gary McIntosh, which focuses on a church's lifecycle, is *Taking your Church to the Next Level*. Gary's ability to communicate, as well as the diagnostics supplied at the end of each chapter, bring a complete understanding to the realities of your church's lifecycle. This is a must-read and is one of the most popular books in my coaching network.

Let me briefly describe the five basic parts of a church's lifecycle. This is critical to your understanding because the next portion of the book is built on this information. There is a reverse lifecycle to leading a turnaround church, and the lifecycles directly correlate to each other.

Knowing where your church is at in its lifecycle will help you strategize how best to lead it through the maze of confusion. It will also give you hope to see that these stages are predictable. Recognizing the characteristics of each phase is important. As you look at the diagram of the lifecycle, don't be discouraged, because a church can grow at any stage of the journey. Most turnaround churches will be in either the fourth or fifth phases of this diagram. Those are the hardest phases to grow from, but it can happen. So don't feel trapped. Your church can move forward.

Our church was started in 1938, making it 57 years old when I arrived in 1995. As I've mentioned, we had dropped from 2,000 to 350 people in average Sunday attendance, and we continued to trend downward for the next ten years, bottoming out at 175 people in attendance each week. I would have put us in the last third of the last phase. We estimated then that we had five to ten years before going out of business.

One of the reasons I'm optimistic about turnaround churches and turnaround pastors is that if a turnaround can happen in Seattle, one of the most unchurched cities in America, it can happen anywhere.

However, in order for a turnaround to happen, there must be a dream of a better day. That is the primary calling of a turnaround pastor, to be the carrier of the vision of that better day, to remind others that the better day is coming, and more importantly, to believe it deeply in your own heart.

Here is a brief overview of the stages of a church's lifecycle.

STAGE 1: THE DREAM

Every church starts with a dream placed by God in someone's heart. Even if a team started a church, there is always a leader.

A man named Hallie Mackey started our church. He was a young, 38-year-old contractor who wanted to start a Sunday school in North Seattle. He was the driving force and the carrier of the dream for many years, although he was never the pastor. He died in 1983, at the age of 83, and also at the church's height in terms of attendance. He saw the church grow, purchase property in North Seattle, and even launch other churches. It must have been very satisfying for him to watch.

Interestingly, his wife never attended church with him. She stayed in her home church of Hollywood Temple in Seattle (now Calvary Christian Assembly).

During the Dream stage, a church usually has rented or borrowed facilities. Very rarely does it have the financial resources to buy or build. But what they do have is a dream, which lends itself to some very positive morale. People are supportive and helpful, and everyone seems to be on task.

There is a general feeling that everyone has to be involved to make this initiative of a new church work. It is not unusual in the early stages of a new church for everyone who goes there to have not only a task but two or three tasks each. People who come with a consumer mentality, to see what the church can offer them, are sadly disappointed and usually leave or never return after the first visit.

There is no youth group or youth pastor, no choir and no worship pastor. In fact the list of what this new church doesn't have is longer that what it does have. Part of the reason there is such focus on the dream of a new church is that no one really knows the future. They all have a hope of what could happen, but no one really knows for sure, so the demand for vision, provided through the pastor, is critical.

There is very little organization, and most decisions are made on the spot without committees. The congregation is very flexible, and goals seem to be quickly accomplished—partly because everyone is involved, and partly because everyone seems to know the limitations. They tackle things they know they can accomplish first. They have no history of failure, so everything becomes a success.

Attendance in this stage varies but almost never breaks 200, and often it's below 100. This group resembles a family reunion, with everyone knowing each other, and every Sunday is like a family gathering. This provides a great sense of belonging to those who are "in" but creates a distinctive barrier to guests and newer attenders. It is not uncommon for someone to attend for a year or more before feeling like they belong, and even then they are usually a relative or friend of someone on the "inside."

A visionary pastor leads this group, at least initially. In some cases the founding pastor knows he will not be the pastor to lead this church to maturity. His assignment is to launch and secure the spiritual beachhead for a new church. Then he will move on after two to five years and perhaps found another church.

It is also possible that founding pastors may envision themselves staying for an extended period of time and leading the church to maturity, but maybe that doesn't work out. Perhaps personal issues, financial pressure, or lack of training simply grind them down, and they have to get out of the church just to survive.

Then there are the pastors who are in this for the long haul. These are pastors who are able to continually resource themselves at every growth junction and keep leading. This is even harder than it appears, but it can and does happen.

More often than not, the first phase of a church's lifecycle concludes with it being about a decade old and the second or third pastor leaving, which opens the door to a new future.

STAGE 2: THE ESTABLISHED CHURCH

During stage two, the church has a track record. It has probably existed between ten and twenty years now with a strong sense of mission. This means those who attend this church have sacrificed to some degree to help get it to this point. There is ownership at a heart level in this church.

Often the church has purchased land or even built by this phase, and they may even have a master plan. There is a sense that they are gaining traction, and they can map out a growth pattern. If a church is going to break the mystical (or even mythical) 200 barrier, it will usually happen during this phase.

This second stage demands that the church be responsive to needs represented in the gathering, so both budget and structure will reflect this adaptation. This is the season when the pastor will introduce more than one adult class, a small group system, or even multiple services.

The church will wrestle through the question of children's ministries. Kids used to come into the service during the music, and now they go to their ministry area before the service begins. Regular youth ministry happens, and outreach is more formalized through intentional big days, to which people are encouraged to invite friends.

These issues are critical because the church is moving from being a bigger "family-reunion" church, with moderate influence, to a higher level of influence in the community. This changes the social structure of the church. There may be resistance with words like, "It doesn't feel like we are a family anymore," or, "There are so many new people around here." But neither of these phrases are said in an encouraging way.

People are sensing the changes, and some have a desire to go back to "the way we used to do things." Their assumption is that we can grow as a church and not change the way we do business, but that isn't true. The average person in a church believes that growth means more people but can't perceive the structure changes required for a church of 125 "simply" growing to 250.

If the leadership, meaning primarily the pastor, cannot navigate this season, especially as the pressure mounts from resisters, then the church will stay just under the 200 barrier, gaining a few new people, and also losing a few people, each year.

If the church continues to make decisions based on "what our people want" or "the kind of church we want to be," then it will not continue to grow. Only mission-based decisions will move it forward. This means that the question is not, "What kind of church do we want?" Rather, it is, "What is the Kingdom potential that Jesus is calling us to?"

This church must be about lost people and reaching them. That is the cause worth our sacrifice and devotion. Accepting Christ's mission is the difference between a church moving the Kingdom of Christ forward or being another Christian club.

The good news is that at this stage the church has momentum with it. If there were ever a time in this church's history that it could break barriers and make the needed changes, it is now.

STAGE 3: MAXIMUM EFFECTIVENESS

This stage is about both effectiveness and efficiency. I have borrowed the term *efficiency* from Charles Arn, author of *How to Start a New Service*. Dr. Arn did extensive research on launching new services and how that interfaces with a church's lifecycle. The church is effective when it is doing the right things. It is efficient when it is doing things right.

Maximum effectiveness means the church has reached its highest visibility and prominence to date. Everyone in the church understands the mission and has bought into it. Additionally, new people rapidly get on board with the focus and purpose of the church. Excitement builds, and momentum increases. If you have ever experienced this stage as a pastor, you know it is a rare and precious season not to be squandered.

During this stage, decisions are easily reached, and unity is high. The church has increasing resources of both people and money. New programs and ministries are started with ease, and volunteers are relatively easy to secure. New members find a place to serve, and new ideas are fostered.

A wise pastor will understand that this is a season, a stage, and it will not last unless new structures are put into place. Usually, the church's governance must change during this stage, and few people are called upon to make more decisions.

The idea of many decisions, let alone every decision, being made by the congregation is long gone. I have trouble thinking of something that will slow down the growth of a church faster than jamming up the decision-making process by allowing everyone, or even many, to make key decisions. The sheer volume of information that must be understood to make a decision at this level is hard to grasp. The pastor and leadership team must possess an understanding of the church trends and why they are this way. Who is the church attracting and why? What is the breakdown of the finances, not just expenses but also income?

At this stage it is not enough to just enjoy the resources God is giving you. You must work at knowing what you need to know. You are leading a cause-based organization, and most of your governing board is probably involved in profit-based organizations. The two are totally different. For a church, the financial bottom line is not the bottom line.

For example, in a profit-based company, if sales are up, you then hire more people to service your customers and hope sales continue to increase. In a church, you first hire the people to develop ministries that will attract others and meet a need, and this is financed by contributions. Can you see why church leadership is much more risky?

I have observed that every time an organization doubles in size, it triples in administration. So at this stage the pastor becomes more manager/leader than leader/manager. When a church grows from 100 to 200, the information has increased but is still manageable. When a church grows from 200 to 400, or 400 to 800, we now have a completely different situation.

The pastor's life is now filled with meetings, ratios, statistics, and metrics, and if the pastor can't get comfortable with that, it will restrict that pastor's ministry. Every ratio represents people and ministry. Not only must the pastor be comfortable with the volume of information, so must the leadership teams of staff, elders, and deacons. Simply put, we are not a "small church" anymore.

If you are pastoring a church in this stage and you hit a snag, then choosing to focus on the mission of reaching lost people, doing what is necessary to move that mission forward, will often get you the right answers. Yes, there is more to risk, decisions take longer, more people are involved, and you have greater consequences. But the mission remains. If the mission of reaching lost people is sacrificed, then the downward spiral begins.

The danger in this stage is that the focus can become more about being efficient than effective. If a church starts asking, "How best can we do things?" that question signals a change in focus and culture. A growing, mission-based church will ask, "What things should we do for the sake of the mission?" The efficient church has moved from the *What* to the *How*. The shift is subtle but significant.

If this local church forgets that Christ died and founded His church to reach lost people through us, then it is comfortable, and that means it's in deep trouble. The church is comfortable because the path of least resistance is being followed. It is in trouble because the mission has now been sacrificed for the goals of this group alone. Our eyes are no longer looking to the fields ready for harvest.

Warning: During this stage I believe that God would love for us to live up to our Kingdom potential as leaders, moving from the Maximum Effectiveness stage to a new Dream stage, but that is usually not what happens. The next stage is what most churches drift into—slowly, quietly, and sadly. Ours surely did.

STAGE 4: THE INSTITUTIONALIZED CHURCH

The fourth stage of a church's lifecycle is institutionalization, which means routine rules the culture and mission has been lost. This is a toxic element being introduced into the church, and if not dealt with, it will eventually kill the church. The longer the church focuses on routine, the more institutionalized it becomes, and the sicker it becomes.

In this stage, the people in the church don't know they are in trouble. All the regular attenders are very content. As author and consultant Lyle Schaller said, "The most comfortable church to be in is a slightly declining church" (See *44 Steps Up Off the Plateau*).

No radical decisions are made, and the focus of the church is maintenance. The dream is long gone, but it doesn't appear to be gone, because there is a building in place, a pastor, and often staff. Each Sunday, the routine goes on with singing, preaching, and offering. Week after week things appear to be normal. Some people have a memory of better days when the church had a mission, but they rarely bring them up because of the tension it would cause.

Since maintenance ministry has replaced a mission focus, very few people are now coming to Christ, and baptisms are fewer, being mostly children. The church still wants to focus on things that matter but not on lost people, so other options begin to surface.

In our history, as I read through the minutes, we were very

mission-focused in the 1960s, but that gave way to a focus on political action. There was a time when the church leadership picketed abortion clinics, and being arrested was a badge of honor. I am certainly not in favor of abortion, and political action may be necessary, but to focus on that instead of the mission of the gospel is off-course.

The next mission diversion we had during the Institutionalized stage was Christian education in place of public education. Again, I am not against Christian schools, but to create a Christian school and think you are doing the mission of the gospel is wrong. You are educating kids in a Christian worldview, and that is good, but it is not the primary mission of the church. This was so prevalent in our church that we sacrificed greatly early on to save the school, as if we were saving the church. Our mission for the gospel had been hijacked, and it needed to be reclaimed.

During the Institutionalized stage, the mission is not passed on to new Christians—because there are very few new Christians—and the seasoned veterans of the gospel have adopted a maintenance ministry stance. The corporate goal is now to provide a tension-free atmosphere, and leaders are selected who will make that happen.

Very few changes occur during this stage, as implied by the word *maintenance*. People who have a passion to spread the gospel or see the church regain its purpose are pressured to conform or leave. Although the institutionalized church wants to live tension-free, there is an abiding tension just below the surface that most can feel but can't describe.

The institutionalized church is the embodiment of *status quo*. This Latin term, meaning *the state in which*, was used in 1853 to explain how the different religious sects should function, when each claimed rights to the Church of the Holy Sepulchre. The agreement was reached after significant violence occurred from the various groups claiming control. Now each group is allowed entrance for a set time and then must exit. Nothing must change. It must remain *status quo*.

The institutionalized church thinks that *status quo* is safe, but it is anything but safe. The church is an army. We are at war, and we are to be on a mission. Anytime a church thinks it can go on R&R for a decade or so, and just remain the same, it is in trouble. A church in maintenance mode is not safe, nor does it glorify God.

Focusing on just maintenance is not about size but attitude. If you pastor a church in a small rural town, loving the people and leading those to Christ who hear the message, that is not maintenance. Your church may never explode, but you are moving the Kingdom faithfully forward, one life at a time.

But if you say in your heart, *This is a small town. Not much will happen here. I'll just put in my time*, this is the language of death.

If it seems that I am particularly direct here, it is because this is a stage when decline can be reversed—if the leaders of a declining church will choose to do so. But that decision takes great humility because you must admit that you need to turn around. You can't make a change unless you admit you need a change, either personally or as a church.

But because it is so hard to admit decline, most churches drift into the last stage.

STAGE 5: THE DISINTEGRATING CHURCH

During the Institutionalized stage, the church was sick and didn't know it. But during the Disintegrating stage, the decline can no longer be ignored. Everybody knows something is wrong, but few know what to do about it.

The most notable characteristics of a disintegrating church are usually finances and facilities. These are often the telltale signs that this church's best days are behind it, unless significant intervention occurs. Most of the people in a disintegrating church have been there many years and are there today because of friendship, not the church's mission.

If you were to ask them what the purpose of the church was, they would give you some version of this phrase: "The church provides a community of faith for us to care for one another." While that answer is not bad, and caring for one another is certainly part of the church's responsibility, it is not the prime directive Jesus gave us.

We are to make disciples and reach the lost, or the whole concept of caring for one another becomes an act of selfishness. The members of a social club care for one another, but do so without the gospel. Caring for one another in a church is important, but it is not the first priority.

In a disintegrating church, programs are cancelled for lack of funding, and 90 percent of the work is done by 10 percent of the people. Leaders are frustrated, not knowing what to do to reverse the obvious trend, and the primary goal becomes survival. If *maintenance* was the key word in the Institutionalized stage, then certainly *survival* is the key word in the Disintegrating stage.

Survival is so important that nothing is risked and no changes are considered that would create frustration. If tension is avoided in the Institutionalized stage, then it is run from in the Disintegrating stage. *Survival* means that nearly every decision is made from a basis of fear and not faith. Jesus can't possibly smile on that.

I grew up with a clear understanding that God wanted us to be faithful, but the Scriptures teach that we are also to be fruitful. In the parable of the talents (Matthew 25), the man who dug a hole and buried his talent was rebuked because he made a decision based on fear. The Lord told him, "You should have done something, anything—even given the talent for others to use. But you did nothing."

Someday we will each stand before Christ and give an account of how we used the talents He gave us. Trying to simply survive paralyzes us, and we make poor decisions because they are based in fear. But we do not have to be ruled by fear, either personally or as a church.

The good news is that Jesus knows how to "strengthen that which remains" and give us a new day. He knows how to help us re-engage with the mission He's assigned us and how to gain a new vision for a better day. That is the journey Jesus invites us to join Him on. It is an adventure of challenges, but what better way to invest your life?

Imagine you are in heaven, talking with Peter and Paul, hearing them retell the stories you've read, and then they both turn and look at you and say, "What did you do to move the Kingdom forward?" And you answer, "Well, I always made sure my church stayed on budget."

Jesus has more for you than that. Jesus has more for your church than where you are now. Let's move His Kingdom forward together.

◄ TURNAROUND PHASE 1 ►
INDUCTION

IN THE SAME WAY THAT A BELL CURVE REPRESENTS the image of a church's lifecycle, a reverse bell curve represents the pathway for a turnaround pastor. It is not a smooth path. It is not always a clear path. But it is a path that can be tracked and, to a degree, planned out, so you can identify some leadership milestones.

The phases of healing and resurrection the church will go through are sometimes indistinguishable until you have passed through them. There is both forward and reverse movement on this pathway, and further, you can show forward progress in some areas and be completely stuck in others.

For example, you can be moving forward in adjusting your church's culture, using worship as the tool for that adjustment, and be lagging in both numerical growth and finances. You can also leap forward with your finances, only to have them slip back during a crucial season because of a key leadership decision.

There is no silver bullet to leading a turnaround church, but the good news is that the master of resurrection, Jesus Himself, is calling you to do this. He has been helping His pastors through tough seasons for centuries, and He does know the pathway. He will lead you clearly if you'll stay connected to Him like a branch to a vine.

Here is visual of the turnaround process. This process can go both forward and backward, but the goal is to keep moving forward. Forward motion is maintained as mission-driven decisions are made. The church feels the greatest tension during the deepest phases of the cycle. These high-tension phases carry the greatest risk of derailing the process and require both intentional and compassionate leadership.

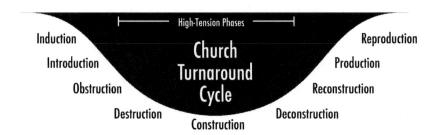

The first phase is Induction, meaning you are now in the game. You have signed up and are in the orientation stage of your leadership. You have the position but virtually no influence.

A new pastor is often brought in to lead a declining church with great hope placed in him or her to lead the church to better days. This places unusually high, and often unrealistic, expectations on this pastor.

I once interviewed with a turnaround church in Oregon. It had dropped in attendance from 150 to nearly 40, and one board member had stepped in and bought the church's mortgage. As you might guess, he was not just the primary interviewer of the new pastoral candidates; he was the only one interviewing. He wanted a new pastor to help the church grow so he could get paid back what he had loaned to the church. I politely declined the offer.

Here is a key to beginning a turnaround: During the interview process, you were asked about your dream for this church, and you shared it. Do not think you are now ready to implement your vision! I failed in my first turnaround church because of this fact. I thought I was ready to start vision-casting without first building a strong relational platform. Building this relational platform is critical. As a turnaround pastor, you are going to make some changes that will bring tension and pressure into the life of this church, and they have to trust you.

Obviously, changes need to be made, or the church would not be in decline, but not everyone agrees that changes need to be made, even if the leadership community has said so. So be smart and build key relationships first. Set your agenda aside, and look for agenda items from others that you can use toward what Jesus has called you to do.

I used to think that everyone responded to an exciting vision, but that is not true. Saints who are older than you want to know you genuinely care about them. For them you are more of a chaplain than a commander; hospital visits, funerals, and weddings are influence-building milestones that cannot be ignored.

During this time, you should also be scouting out the influencers in the church and building relationships with them. They are the ones who will ultimately help you do Jesus' agenda here, but they must first learn you are trustworthy. There is no substitute for quality time with these church leaders. Every successful turnaround pastor knows the value of building key relationships.

If you think this is just church politics, you are totally missing the point of building key relationships. If there is something inside you that says, *I'm God's man with God's plan, and our people should just recognize that*, well, keep your résumé tuned up.

I remember meeting with Ed, who was the key lay leader in our church for years before I got there and for several years after I came. We had a weekly breakfast for the first three years, and we talked about everything. When an item needed to be discussed and decided at an elders' meeting, we both knew where the other stood on the subject.

Often his support provided the tipping point to some crucial decisions, such as raising money to upgrade our worship space, moving to multiple services, and trading out our pews for chairs. All of those decisions were impacting points on our church's culture, and I needed key lay leaders to help me.

A church in the Induction phase is like the walking dead. Their sense of mission is dead; their vision for the future is dead; and they have focused so long on just surviving that their endurance may be close to dead. Declining churches have a big rearview mirror and a very small windshield. For most people in plateaued or declining churches, they believe the best days of their church are behind them, but they want to believe better days could be ahead. They also want to believe that you are going to help get them there, but they are unsure.

Working through this phase will take you the better part of a year, maybe more. Building relationships takes a while, but you have time. If Jesus called you here, you always have enough time to do God's will. And certainly building solid, trustworthy relationships is a key to turning a church around.

During the Induction phase, you need to gather information about the church's history. Ask questions about the past and take good notes. The fact that you are asking older saints and established people in the church will put you in good standing. People are honored when we listen to them.

When you meet with people, listen to the stories of the glory days. Ask questions about how events and people intersected with the life of the church. If the previous pastor left under bad circumstances, which is very common, be sure to be respectful and hold your opinions of his or her leadership to yourself.

Remember that a church with a long history, especially a declining church, has deep institutional memory. Institutional memory is a collection of facts and experiences that hold this group together. It is often passed down to new members and even new generations. A wise turnaround pastor will access this institutional memory and look for repeated stories. These stories will reflect the current values of this church.

Whenever possible, use these stories in your preaching, especially your first year. This will illustrate that you are listening. You will find yourself being further welcomed into this community.

Institutional memory also has a downside. It is institutional memory that produces such statements as, "We've never done that before," or, "We've tried that before, and it didn't work." Either way, institutional memory is a two-edged sword, so it cannot be ignored.

One of the most important efforts you can make in this time is to understand the key to each leader's life. John Maxwell teaches on this idea in his book *The Five Levels of Leadership*, and you will gain an important understanding of the leadership process by reading it.

Understanding the key to a leader's life means knowing what is important to them personally. Whether it's a hobby or an activity or a relationship, take note and ask them about it from time to time. Your interest in their life is not only caring; it sows good seed for the time when you will need their support for what is important in your life. You will reap what you sow.

During the Induction phase, you are becoming acquainted with those you will lead. At the same time, you know that some of them will also leave you through death, transfer, or irritation. That is a part of leadership, but pour your life into them anyway. Jesus did.

If pastoral trust is low—and that is a common factor in the Induction phase—taking time to build key relationships will help you move forward. You will be able to build trust through consistency and compassion over time. Yes, this will take time, lots of time, so choose to be patient with yourself and your people. Remember, Jesus is being patient with you.

INDUCTION REFLECTION QUESTIONS

1. How long have you been the pastor of your current church? (If more than three years, you are probably past the Induction phase.)

2. If your church's average weekly attendance is under 100, who are your top three influencers? If your church's average weekly attendance is 100–200, who are your top four to six influencers? If your church's average weekly attendance is 200–500, who are your top 10 influencers?

3. How have you built relationships with each of your church's influencers?

4. Do you have an idea of the "key" to their life? What are the important issues for each of your leaders?

5. Graph out the last three to five years of both giving and attendance at your church. What does this tell you? How do the spikes or dips on the graphs coincide with the stories you have heard from the institutional memories of those in your church?

6. List five to 10 key points, experiences, or decisions of your church's institutional memory that are critical to your understanding. Why do you think they are so important to your people?

7. What is your basic understanding as to why your church is in decline? Why do your leaders think it is in decline? How is your assessment different than your church's leadership community?

8. Through your conversations, what are some ideas, projects, or ministries you've discovered that you can champion? How will you champion them?

9. Write out at least 10 of your church's expectations of you as the pastor now. Which ones excite you? Why? Which ones frustrate you? Why?

10. Do you have a clear sense that Jesus wants you to lead this church through a turnaround? How do you know this is your Kingdom assignment?

11. What personal obstacles do you face as you prepare to lead your church?

12. What will you focus your prayers on during this first phase? List the areas you will regularly cover in prayer.

13. List out any Scriptures Jesus has put in your heart to strengthen your leadership during this phase of the turnaround.

◄ TURNAROUND PHASE 2 ►
INTRODUCTION

"HELL IS HOT, AND FOREVER IS A LONG TIME." I watched the words move across my computer screen. My screensaver had kicked on, and I'd put these words there to remind me why our church existed. It was my first week on the job, and I wanted some kind of regular reminder to keep me mission-focused.

I had finished giving my first sermon as the new pastor and had introduced the concept that all of our friends, neighbors, and relatives were either lost or saved. It seemed simple enough to me, and it was certainly the central theme of the gospel; but it fell upon ears that were not used to hearing such messages.

As I sat down next to my associate, Richard Vicknair, he leaned over to me and said, "Everything you say is marinated in the gospel. You must think people are more interested in hearing the gospel than most of us have experienced."

I had just introduced a central theme that would propel our church forward in the years to come, but at this moment, it had very little effect. No one disagreed with me, but the idea that the people sitting in these pews were actually going to talk to other people about the gospel, even people they knew, seemed highly unlikely.

The Introduction phase is where you, as the leader, begin introducing the idea that the church can and should move beyond a survival mentality. You must do this even if you are still declining numerically, which you probably are. Your church needs to hear the idea that the church does not exist for itself alone. In fact, the local church does not exist for itself primarily. The local church exists for the purpose of doing the mission of God, and that means your church exists more for non-members than for members.

As you lead through this phase, you shouldn't expect any open applause or pastoral cheering sections. You are raising the tension in this church simply by talking like this, but that must happen. It is only when we understand how the gospel impacts us personally that we begin to change. When we understand that we are responsible to share Christ with our neighbor, friend, and co-worker, then the gospel becomes personal. When the gospel becomes personal to me, I must do something. I must either comply and obey, or resist and disobey; there is no third option. That raises tension.

During this phase, you are telling your church in love and compassion, but clearly, that their season as a Christian club is over. The days when we all got together because we just loved getting together, when teaching and preaching was an excuse, are simply over. We are on a mission.

During this phase there are three key introductions you will have to make to your church. These introductions can't happen through a single sermon, but they will have to come through your teaching for sure. More specifically, they will be introduced through leadership conversations you will have with your staff, deacons, and elders, as well as influential leaders in your church. In this phase, you'll need to introduce:

1. A Biblical Basis for Outreach

2. A Compelling Mission

3. Tenacious Leadership

INTRODUCING A BIBLICAL BASIS FOR OUTREACH

Introducing biblical information on the Great Commission and outreach will be the easiest and most obvious because people will expect it—and they should. The disconcerting part is that, as pastors, we think that when we say something, people hear us. It doesn't take too many years in ministry before we know that is just not the case. People have been trained for years to hear God's Word and do nothing. Does this surprise anyone?

Nevertheless, you will need to teach the biblical basis for reaching out. You'll have to teach that God is serious about reaching lost people, so we need to be serious too. Here are a few passages to help you get started:

For the Son of Man came to seek and to save the lost.
Luke 19:10

And I tell you that you are Peter, and on this rock I will build
my church, and the gates of Hades will not overcome it.
Matthew 16:18

...that everyone who believes may have eternal life in him.
John 3:15

The Lord is not slow in keeping his promise, as some under-
stand slowness. Instead he is patient with you, not wanting
anyone to perish, but everyone to come to repentance.
II Peter 3:19

I urge, then, first of all, that petitions, prayers, intercession
and thanksgiving be made for all people, for kings and all
those in authority, that we may live peaceful and quiet lives
in all godliness and holiness. This is good, and pleases God
our Savior, who wants all people to be saved and to come to a
knowledge of the truth.
I Timothy 2:1–4

But you'll need to do more than just teach to introduce the concept of the Great Commission. You'll need to link teaching and action. Don't do this alone. You'll miss a great opportunity to invite people on the journey if you do the planning alone and only come up with your own ideas. Instead, gather three to eight people with you and ask them, "How can we take this concept and put it into practice?"

Most plateaued and declining churches have very few guests, or they wouldn't be declining. So reaching out to people is key. Here are some ways that we reached out while simultaneously teaching on making disciples.

Win Arn and Charles Arn wrote *The Master's Plan for Making Disciples*, in which they describe the *"oikos* principle.*" Oikos* is the Greek word for *household*, but don't think *family*; think *relational network*. When the Apostle Paul said to the Philippian jailer in Acts 16:31, "Believe in the Lord Jesus, and you will be saved—you and your household," he wasn't just talking about the jailer's immediate family. He was referring to anyone with whom the jailer had a relationship. Arn states that most people know six to eight people who are outside the gospel. If you have your Sunday congregation add up the names of everyone they know, you now have a "potential congregation." And those names represent the people closest to your church's influence.

I did a study over several Sundays, searching out the New Testament uses of the word *household*. During that time we came up with a couple of ideas that made it personal and got our people involved. First, one Sunday I had a sheet placed in the Sunday bulletin that said, "My Extended Spiritual Family," with lines numbered 1–10 where people could write the names of family members, friends, and relatives who did not know Christ and were not a part of our church. We then had everyone turn in their paper, and we added up the names.

I explained that because we already have a trusted relationship with these people, they are open to the gospel. Everyone agreed, but very few did anything. At the time, I had high hopes that they would start sharing Christ with others, but that just didn't happen. There is an axiom in counseling that says, "Past behavior is the best predictor of future performance." That is true with the church too. They weren't bad people. They loved Jesus. But the mission of the gospel had not yet penetrated their hearts. Church was still for them and maybe a few others. Nevertheless, the point was made: everyone in the church knew at least some lost people.

We took another shot at using the *oikos* principle. We developed prayer cards with eight lines on one side to write down the names of friends and neighbors who were far from Christ. I encouraged the congregation to put these cards in their pockets and purses and pray for their friends as God brought the friends to mind. Some of them did.

Then something happened that helped us gain traction. During a series on the seven churches of Revelation, we started taking communion every Sunday. I wasn't sure this was a good idea. But then I remembered that Seattle is a very Catholic city, and Catholics are used to taking communion every week. So we switched to weekly communion, and the idea gained traction. To this day, we receive communion in every service.

About that time, our team came up with the idea for both a motto and a practice that would keep the mission of the gospel in front of us. In our services, people come to tables around the perimeter of the room to take the communion elements. Behind each table, we hung a large white sheet of paper. We placed the motto *Every Conversation Counts* in the center of the paper, to remind people that the connections they make really matter.

On each communion table was a basket of large Sharpie markers. Each Sunday, when the people came forward for communion, we encouraged them to write down the first name of anyone new they had met that week. And they did. In four months' time, we collected over 800 names from this church of 175 people.

We encouraged many other ideas in connection with our teaching. For two months, we encouraged our people to invite their neighbors over for dinner, with no agenda, but to bless the meal together and perhaps ask their neighbors if there was anything they would like prayer for. We've hosted several neighborhood barbecues and even sponsored "Operation Kindness," where we asked our neighbors in advance about practical needs we could meet, like small home repairs, and then sent out teams during the Sunday service to help them.

These kinds of actions are necessary and will produce some fruit, but the real value is in shifting the culture, which happens incrementally in a turnaround church. In the Introduction phase, you are helping your church get outside the box and start thinking about lost people. That is the real value of such exercises. You'll actually begin to see the church grow when new people bring other new people, but that is a few phases down the road.

People will come to Christ during this phase, though. Robert is a good example. One day he just showed up with his three children. Soon after he received Christ, joined a small group, and began to grow spiritually. I later learned that he was the regional vice president for a large company, and he oversaw about 1,200 employees. As the gospel took root in his life, tensions at work and at home increased, but he stood strong. He ended up losing both his job and his marriage, but Jesus sustained him. Robert continues to be a part of Creekside Church to this day. He is a reminder of the fruit of the gospel during a difficult time.

INTRODUCING A COMPELLING MISSION

During the Introduction phase, a turnaround pastor is confronting the fact that the people in the church are uninformed about Jesus' mandate to the disciples. Talking to your church about the mission of the church is a must during this phase. It begins with a review of Christ's Great Commission.

> Then Jesus came to them and said, "All authority in heaven and on earth has been given to me. Therefore go and make disciples of all nations, baptizing them in the name of the Father and of the Son and of the Holy Spirit, and teaching them to obey everything I have commanded you. And surely I am with you always, to the very end of the age."
> Matthew 28:18–20

When I say that your people are uninformed, I'm not saying they don't know about these verses or know that the church is supposed to be reaching out. Most of them know both the verses and the concept, but it hasn't affected personal behavior. Otherwise, the church would not be in decline.

The best tool I know for turning a church outward is the development of a mission statement that will be emotionally embraced by the whole church.

One pastor who led a turnaround church took his church through the process of developing a mission statement, and then he actually carried that document around for three years. Every time a leader engaged him in conversation with the intent to shift the church focus in another direction, he would pull out that document and say, "This is the mission we agreed upon as a church. Let's stick to it." As a result, he saw the church rebound from 35 people each week to its previous 150 and then far beyond, to several thousand people attending each week. A church that is truly sold out to a Christ-centered mission is a powerful force for Christ in a community.

How do you develop a mission statement? As you begin to help your church focus on developing a mission statement, it is important to keep in mind that the process is more important than the product.

Almost every church's mission statement is restating Christ's Great Commission in some way. For your church to own this statement, they must emotionally embrace it. That means you'll have to go through some kind of process that allows these leaders to make significant contributions, or they will never feel like it is their statement. Too many pastors have crafted good mission statements in their office, but the statements never got off the ground because they were not emotionally embraced or owned in the hearts of other leaders.

There is a lot of material out there on developing a mission statement, but here are a few simple guidelines:

1. Make sure it is biblical. Obviously, you will need to create a biblical foundation, and the best way to do this is through a simple Bible study with your key influencers, whether they are in a position of leadership or not. Take them through the Bible, and show the key passages that focus on the church as God's way to reach lost people.

   You'll need to give a good two months to this process to bond the team to this purpose. Any shorter and you won't elicit enough responses to hear what is really in their hearts. Don't rush this. Let your leaders do most of the talking while you ask questions. This is not the time for you to teach but to listen. Listening is much more influential than talking.

2. Start with lots of words. After you've met together for a while, ask this question, "Why does our church exist?" A mission statement should answer that question. Then write down every response from everyone. Don't worry about it being too long. The value here is that everyone is contributing, so make sure everyone actually contributes.

   During this phase, our leadership team filled up an entire 6'x4' whiteboard with words. I wanted the leaders to be able to look up to the board and see their words up there.

   Also, it will probably be your hope, since you've been leading a Bible study on outreach, asking about outreach, and discussing outreach, that most of the people's responses to this question will be outreach-oriented responses. That probably won't be the case.

When you ask them about why the church exists, they will hear, "What do I need from the church?" This the normal screening process a group will go through, so be patient and let the leaders catch up with you.

3. End with very few words. Now it's time to refine and focus your mission statement. Begin by asking if every line or phrase is necessary. Then ask if every word is necessary. Try to refine and boil it down to its fundamental essence. A mission statement is only useful if it is used, and it will not be used if you can't remember it. You'll only remember it if it is short enough to remember. I suggest a mission statement be less than ten words. Ours is eight words.

Be sure you, as the pastor, can believe and support this statement. If you acquiesce or give in to please others, this mission statement will not be the tool you need to lead a turnaround. You also need to let your leaders have input too. This is a balancing act, but it can be done—and you'll need to lead it.

4. Build support. Now that the leadership community of your church has bought into and helped develop a mission statement, it's time to get the rest of the church on board. Imagine that you are working through concentric circles, starting with your most influential leaders, then other ministry leaders, and finally the church as a whole.

Mission Statement Process

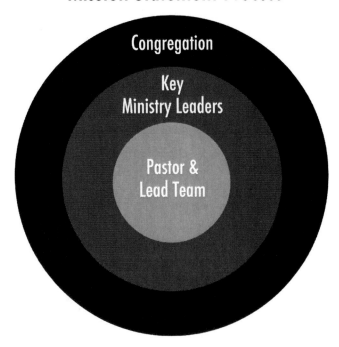

You've now spent two to four months working with your most influential leaders to develop this statement. Now it is time to include other ministry leaders to get buy-in from them. Ideally, they already know what is going on because your most influential leaders have been leaking information to them throughout the process. You will probably only need a meeting or two for group input to get traction with this extended group. Be sure to include your most influential leaders, and add these other ministry leaders to the mix. This way, the entire leadership community will be leading, not just you.

Then take it to the church. We did this with a simple survey, listing the statement and asking people to write *yes* or *no*. Again, most of those in the church were familiar with it before we went public, thanks to our strategic info-leaking.

USING YOUR MISSION STATEMENT

Your mission statement is worthless to you as leader if you don't use it and use it often. Robert Logan, author of *Beyond Church Growth*, stated that a church can lose its focus in as little as one month if not reminded of its mission. In a turnaround church it can happen sooner. In a turnaround church there is incredible pull back to its unproductive past, so use your mission statement weekly.

It should be on your program, on the wall, and in any other place that seems prudent. You will need to use it as a filter in your boardroom, where decisions should be made based on whether they move the mission forward or not. Use your mission statement in hiring staff, setting the budget, and especially in your preaching. If you are not pointing to your mission as part of Christ's mission, why would anyone sacrifice, give, or work for it? As the leader, how you cast vision toward a compelling mission is critical.

INTRODUCING TENACIOUS LEADERSHIP

As the pastor and leader of a turnaround church, you have been called to reverse the trend. You are here to intervene. Jesus will lead, but you are His mouthpiece. You are to walk humbly and listen well, but then you must lead. If you do not lead, there will be no turnaround, because Jesus is asking you to do this.

Tenacious leadership will not quit. You will get discouraged, but you'll recover. There will be setbacks, but you'll try again. You'll run out of money, but there will be more. People will leave your church, but others will come. Leaders will resist you, but other leaders will thank God for sending you to them. Above all, you must trust Jesus to work through you, and you must not give up.

This means you will have to continually speak life to this declining church and teach that a better day is coming. You will be the one to initiate new ideas and plans. They won't all work, but some of them will. You'll gain traction with every success.

And you'll need to make some courageous decisions that may bring levels of pain into your life and the life of the church. Those decisions are similar to the ones the Lord makes in our life. John 15 tells us He prunes us so more fruit may come.

INTRODUCTION REFLECTION QUESTIONS

1. Do you believe that the primary mission of the church is to reach lost people?

2. List the ways you have communicated, or could communicate, to your church that reaching lost people is the primary mission of your church.

3. Does your church have a grasp of the biblical basis for outreach as its primary focus? How do you know this concept has deeply penetrated your church culture?

4. How have you connected your teaching with outreach activities? Who could serve on an outreach team with you to develop a monthly outreach activity for the next year? List their names and three possible activities or events below. Remember, these activities don't need to be large events, just simple challenges to help people think outside of themselves in their everyday lives.

5. Does your church have a mission statement? If yes, write about the process used to develop it.
   If your church does not have a mission statement, why not? Do you think it is important to have one? Why or why not?

6. Who are the key influential leaders you would need working with you to develop a mission statement? Is there anything that would prevent them from working with you? Can that be overcome?

7. Are you willing to exhibit loving and tenacious leadership for your church? What, if anything, prevents you from leading in this manner now?

8. What will you focus your prayers on during this second phase? List the areas you will regularly cover in prayer.

9. List out any Scriptures Jesus has put in your heart to strengthen your leadership during this second phase of the turnaround.

◄ TURNAROUND PHASE 3 ►
OBSTRUCTIONS

THE OBSTRUCTION PHASE IS THE SEASON when you will see new ideas rise and resistance increase. Resisters will be identified and you will gain a clearer understanding of the challenges you are up against, but don't be discouraged. Jesus has called you to walk this road, and you are not alone. Your obedient pursuit will result in people coming to Jesus, so don't give up. You are confronting sterile, apathetic ministry, and it is hard work. But a better day is coming. Here is a glimpse of my walk through this phase.

I looked at the group assembled to interview me. I was not yet the pastor. I knew I had to be honest with them. I also knew it would be painful. So I responded to the question, "What changes would you make if you came to be our pastor?"

"As you know, I've done some research on this church. Well over half of the people who call this church home are over 60 years of age. If we are honest about reaching people, especially younger people so the church will have a future, then our worship has to get younger and louder."

The groan was audible. A woman in her 70s looked at me and said, "Louder music? It seems like we already have loud music, and we still don't have younger people coming. I don't think that is going to do it."

I replied, "Ann, thank you for your comment. You are right: just singing newer songs and turning up the volume will not get new people streaming through the door, but it has to be a part of the mix, along with many other changes we'll need to consider."

I had just hit my first obstruction, and I wasn't even the pastor yet. Obstructions in ministry are part of the job, but in a turnaround, they can both ambush you and entrap you.

As you may have guessed by now, there is no clear defining line when you leave one phase and enter the next. You actually get a better view as time goes on, so being a turnaround pastor is more art than science.

The phases are also not sequential; you can be in two or three different phases at the same time, in different areas of your ministry. As you can see from the story above, I had bumped into the Obstruction phase, and I wasn't even the pastor yet. But bumping into a phase and moving completely through it are two different things entirely. For example, since worship sets and identifies the culture of a church to a new person more than anything else, the shift in music had to take place. But this was not a decision I made in a boardroom and then executed. I actually contended with our music shift for over six years; it was a major obstruction.

An obstruction is anything that stops, hinders, or detours the accomplishment of your assigned mission. Obstructions must be removed, quarantined, or bypassed. The one thing you cannot do is ignore an obstruction. If you try, it will remain like a boulder in the road, completely halting your progress. The advantage you have as a turnaround pastor is that obstructions announce themselves. They are obvious, which makes them easy to identify—but not necessarily easy to deal with.

Another key point here is that you rarely deal with one obstruction at a time. It is more than likely that you will have to deal with six to 10 obstructions of varying intensity at the same time. Each one will have the power to at least slow you down and maybe even derail you completely.

As you identify and strategize about how to deal with obstructions, remember that God has given you two very powerful tools. Spending time with the Lord in prayer and in His Word will give you guidance; that is your first tool. Your second tool is your mission. You will be able to confront issues of the church's culture because you are on a mission.

In John 4, Jesus has a conversation with a Samaritan woman. In our culture the fact that he has this conversation does not seem like a big deal, but it was a big deal for Jesus' culture. Jews and Samaritans didn't get along, so Jesus actually crossed the cultural lines when he asked her for some water. This opened the door to a mission-based conversation, and she eventually not only accepted Christ but also became a significant evangelist.

Later in the chapter, when Jesus' disciples returned from buying food, they saw him talking with her, but the Scriptures say that none of the disciples asked him about this. Jesus had crossed the cultural lines of his day for the sake of the mission, and those well versed in the culture (his disciples) saw what he was doing.

If they had questions about Jesus' actions, they didn't raise them. But the fact that Jesus had crossed these cultural lines got their attention, at least enough so that John included it in his gospel.

Being on a mission together is extremely powerful. Being on a mission allows you to both confront and, when necessary, cut across cultural lines for the sake of the mission.

You have already led your church through the development of a mission statement, and you cannot forget that. The changes you must make, which will cause the obstructions to surface, must be mission-based changes. They cannot be personal, or they will blow up on you. If you make changes just because you like something, you have now become the savior, and that job is already taken.

Mission-based changes must be clear to all that they move the mission forward. Those who resist may object, but if you do your homework, they will see it. They may never agree, and may even leave the church, but your motivation will be obvious: you believe this decision is best for the sake of the mission.

People resist mission-based decisions because of how it affects them personally. We don't like a 75-minute service if we were raised in a two-hour service. We don't like the offering at the end of the service if we are used to having it in the middle. In short, all of us deal with wanting things our own way. The people in a declining church want to see the church grow; they just don't want anything to change.

An elder once said to me during this season, as we talked about our aged and poorly conditioned church building, "If I invite people to my house, they accept me and my house as it is. I don't feel the need to remodel my house to make people feel comfortable."

He didn't mind if the church grew, meaning more people showing up on a Sunday, but he wouldn't support the initiatives to help us get there. Eventually he left our church, but his words caused another obstruction to surface.

Obviously his argument had holes in it. There is a huge difference between people's expectations of private space, like your home, and public space, like a church. I did not contend with him at this point. It would not have been worth the conflict. I knew that he would eventually leave us, so I chose to endure the tension and spend my energy elsewhere.

This illustrates the first part of dealing with obstructions: You must get them to surface. The good news is that this will happen naturally. All you will have to do is cast vision, and the obstructions will rise.

The second step is to determine whether you will deal with this obstruction now, later, or not at all. Prepare to ignore most of them. You will have minor, moderate, and major obstructions. Dealing with a moderate obstruction will take care of several other minor obstructions at the same time. Dealing with a major obstruction will take care of several moderate-level issues and many minor issues as well.

You will find that Jesus will direct you to deal with the major issues first, which will require courage and obedience, but your efforts will produce the most fruit there. Don't get caught up spending your energy on a bunch of little things or even the moderate things. Go after the big rocks first.

We faced many obstructions turning our church around: our facilities, Christian school, staff, money, worship style, and many others. Each took a different strategy and a significant amount of time.

To deal with our facilities, we made four focused efforts over a 12-year period. Our simple strategy was to have a worship service in the space that needed attention. Not everyone liked what we did, and people left. But other people came. The mission-based vision was as compelling as the facility projects.

We transitioned our Christian school to its own organization over a six-year period of time. Again, I am not against Christian schools. They can be an incredible blessing. The obstacle in our case was that the school had become the mission of the church, and we were sacrificing to continue an entity that won very few people to Christ. Our strategy was to raise the rent on the school until it could pay its own way and become its own legal entity. Then we gave the school four years to find a new home. I think it was generous on our part to take six years to do all this, but not everyone agreed with me. Surprising, huh?

Our staff was somewhat of an obstruction, but not the entire staff. Simply changing staff can be an obstruction because people become bonded to leaders. Every time a leader leaves, the tranquility of the church is disturbed. We averaged laying off, or even firing, one staff member a year for fourteen years. Some were pastors, and others were support staff. I'm not proud of that, but it is what happened. And some of those decisions were incredibly difficult. Again, without a clear mission, I would not have had the fortitude to follow through on these issues, nor would I have had the council's support.

Money in any church can be a real obstacle, but in a turnaround it just feels like it's even more difficult. The truth is, a money issue isn't really a money issue as much as a vision issue. It seems like there is never enough to go around, but I'd like to challenge that concept. Saying there is never enough money is the same as saying there is never enough time, but that isn't true either. We may feel that way about both subjects, but that doesn't make it true.

There is always enough time to do God's will. If it seems there isn't enough time, either we are doing the wrong things or not doing the right things. Either way, it's an issue of obedience, not time. I want to suggest the same is true for money. There is always enough money to do God's will. God has promised that our needs will be met. God has promised that we will have enough to help others and that His church will move forward.

Making sure you are well resourced as a church does not happen overnight, but it can happen. As you build a culture of generosity in your church, you will see things change over time. As you teach your people to give and show responsible management, you will be trusted with more and will overcome the money obstruction.

Of course, you can't lead a generous church without being a generous pastor, and you can't teach your people to give if you don't give also. Leaders reproduce after their own kind. If we're feeling the money pinch, maybe the issue is actually our own obedience as leaders. Maybe we just don't feel comfortable talking about it, so our people are not being led. Now the real obstacle is internal, not external.

Here is a short checklist to see if you are doing what you can as a leader to help your church become well resourced.

1. Do you believe that stewardship is part of discipleship?

2. Do you teach on biblical stewardship at least annually, or even better, quarterly?

3. Do you provide multiple ways of giving beyond your Sunday morning offering (e.g., auto debit, online, giving kiosk, business reply envelopes in the program)?

4. Do you mail out quarterly thank-you letters with giving statements?

5. What kind of preparation do you put into your words regarding the offering portion of your service?

6. Do you send a personal thank-you note to first-time givers?

7. Do you offer a stewardship class or small group to teach people about financial responsibility?

8. Are you a faithful tither and giver yourself?

Regardless of how uncomfortable you feel about money, the subject just can't be ignored. Your church has all you need to accomplish God's will. You have enough time, and you have enough money; just use both wisely and watch what happens.

Shifting our worship style was a long and difficult challenge, but I saw it as a key obstruction that needed to be dealt with. We were singing songs from the 1970s and '80s, and it just wasn't working.

One of the important facts on this subject is well taught in Gary McIntosh's book, *One Church, Four Generations*, where he talks about Builders, Boomers, Busters, and Bridgers. When it comes to worship style, Gary tells us that we come to love and appreciate the music of our own generation, and as new generations rise, that style of worship is challenged. One of the key points we used in helping seniors, or those of both the Builder and Boomer generations, adapt to a new worship style was this focus: "God has called us to reach the generation of your children and grandchildren. We know you may not like this style, but your kids will. So would you be willing to support this change on that basis?"

This struggle went back and forth for years, but over time, we were able to make the shift and see a new culture emerge. Your worship style is critical to your culture. Samuel Chand says in his book *Cracking Your Church's Culture* that culture trumps vision. I believe that to be especially true for a turnaround pastor.

I am suggesting you use vision for what it could be, a tool for adjusting and shifting your culture first. That cultural adjustment will paint a picture over time of your vision for the future and move you forward in your mission.

Now here are some words of warning, as you face obstructions and strategize a course through them. Jesus said in Matthew 10:16, "Be as shrewd as snakes and as innocent as doves." To be a turnaround pastor, you will need to be both shrewd and innocent at the same time.

There are times when you must be overt, as in casting vision and leading publicly. But there are also times to be covert. I don't mean you should be deceptive or dishonest. God will not bless that, but as a leader there are times when you cannot and should not let others in on your thinking. Sometimes you're not totally clear on what to do, or the timing is wrong, or there just isn't the trust yet for you to share all you are thinking. Those are times to be covert and careful, "shrewd as a serpent." Not every situation is safe, and not every person is safe. You need to be as wise as Mary, who "pondered these things in her heart."

OBSTRUCTION REFLECTION QUESTIONS

1. Do you have a clear idea of the mission-based changes needed in your church?

2. List as many obstructions to moving forward in your mission as you can think of.

3. From the list above, rate every obstruction as major, moderate, or minor.

4. Which obstruction is the most difficult for you to deal with, and why?

5. Now prioritize the top three obstructions, and write out a basic strategy for dealing with each one.

6. Find another pastor you trust. Share these three obstructions with them, and let them read your answers without making any comments. Then ask for their feedback. What did you learn from their feedback?

6. What will you focus your prayers on during this third phase? List the areas you will regularly cover in prayer.

7. List out any Scriptures Jesus has put in your heart to strengthen your leadership during this third phase of the turnaround?

INSIGHT FROM LEADERS

One Life Community Church is a 37-year-old church in Seattle. We started off as a church plant ministering to college students at the University of Washington in 1976. Over the years the church grew to its height of about 350 people then the church began to struggle and has been in decline ever since, dropping to 50-60 people on a Sunday.

We knew things needed to change. This is where Don Ross and the Turnaround Church Coaching Network came in. As a church we have now gone through every course offered, twice in the last two years. The results of our experience having gone through these classes are amazing.

Over the last two years we have seen…

- More new people come to our church then the last 12 years.
- We have seen the majority of these new people coming from within a mile of our church.
- We maxed out our parking for our service so we added a new service in January 2013. Since then we have continued to grow steadily to where we are now seeing an average attendance of 215.
- We have seen more new giving units in the last two years then we have seen in the last 12 years.
- We have added over 30 new members to our church and retained 98% of our previous members.
- We retooled our small group ministry structure and just in this last year we have had 30 new people join one or more of our core groups.
- We have never had a formalized tithes and offering time during our services for 37 years. This year for the first time we started doing what we learned in TCCN and our giving has grown and we've made budget for the first time in eight years and have an actual savings.
- We purchased our first building
- With the coaching we received we even took two "special offer-ings" where we brought in close to $20,000 for two of our loved missionaries. Note: this is on top of our regular giving and our regular annual missions budget

- We have been more connected and rooted in our community then we have ever been. We have started a tutoring program ministering to the public schools with over 20+ students we serve each week that are referred to us from the school district.
- We started a community garden that provides vegetables to the local food bank
- We began the process of starting a separate non-profit wellness cooperative providing various professional health services to the community
- We are now connected and trusted by our community counsel and are now asked to help serve the community through this new relationship
- We also see on average another 100+ people from the community coming into our building on a daily basis through better stewardship of our building.

We are amazed at what God is doing in the midst of One Life Community Church. Through Don's coaching and experience we have been consistently challenged every time we meet during class. There was not one session where we did not leave with applications that have helped make our church a healthier place.

On top of all this what is probably even more valuable is the relationships that have formed since being in these classes. Having a space to be honest, accountable, and supported was priceless. Having a great group of pastors to remind you that you are not the only one going through struggles was helpful, but also being able to share our successes each month was so exciting

If you are a pastor of a church that has been in decline and you are looking for some coaching/training/support to help lead it through a turnaround towards health then we could not recommend TCCN classes higher. The teaching, coaching, reading, discussions and the relationships, make for such a perfect learning setting that will change you and your church towards becoming a healthy growing congregation. You will be glad you did!

Pastors Rich Sclafani & Greg Di Loreto
Co Lead Pastors
One Life Community Church, Seattle

◄ TURNAROUND PHASE 4 ►
DESTRUCTION

"I THINK THE TIME HAS COME for us to talk about the leadership of this church, specifically our pastor and where he is taking this church. I am very concerned, and I believe we will have a crisis on our hands if we continue. Now is the time for us to talk about this."

I wasn't totally shocked when this subject came up. I knew some felt this way; I was just surprised at the boldness of this particular elder to introduce such a topic during a council meeting. I could tell from the response of the others that his words had gained some traction. I wasn't sure how to respond.

I had been the pastor for about four years at this point. I knew antagonists were beginning to surface. I had done my best to gain buy-in from the leadership community on the changes we'd made, but I certainly didn't have 100 percent support. Even so, I had made the strategic decision to forge ahead. It boiled down to a matter of obedience.

You know you've hit the Destruction phase when antagonists begin to make their presence known, and you, as the turnaround pastor, must be the one to confront both issues and people. You are becoming the destroyer of the mediocre in order to lead the church into something good, maybe even great.

Let's do a short recap of what we've already discussed:

1. The phases of a turnaround church are not sequential, but they are identifiable, though often only after the fact.

2. You can be in several phases at the same time in different areas of the church.

3. The Induction phase focuses on developing a basic understanding of a declining church's situation, and it often will take the better part of a year to get a sense of history and determine the key players.

4. The Introduction phase focuses on introducing the mission of the gospel to the church, taking them beyond survival, and developing a mission statement. Here you introduce key ministry leadership initiatives that will help adjust the culture.

The Destruction phase focuses on overt changes to the church. You will identify practices and values that hinder the mission and must be eliminated. This is a high-risk phase.

We don't like to think about it, but destruction is always part of moving forward, especially as a turnaround pastor. But this destruction is not random or vindictive. This destruction is about moving forward and being on a mission. Your church will experience some minor destruction in order to have new ministries spring up.

Remodeling a house carries the same understanding. To update an old home, you must first destroy what is there before you can have something new. But you're intentional about it. You wouldn't destroy the bathroom if your goal were to remodel the kitchen. The same is true for a turnaround pastor.

Jesus illustrates this principle well in the story of the rich, young ruler in Mark 10:17–22.

> As Jesus started on his way, a man ran up to him and fell on his knees before him. "Good teacher," he asked, "what must I do to inherit eternal life?" "Why do you call me good?" Jesus answered. "No one is good—except God alone. You know the commandments: 'You shall not murder, you shall not commit adultery, you shall not steal, you shall not give false testimony, you shall not defraud, honor your father and mother.'" "Teacher," he declared, "all these I have kept since I was a boy." Jesus looked at him and loved him. "One thing you lack,"

he said. "Go, sell everything you have and give to the poor, and you will have treasure in heaven. Then come, follow me." At this the man's face fell. He went away sad, because he had great wealth.

In order for this man to have true eternal riches, he would need to be willing to give up temporal riches. He saw this request as destruction in his life and refused to obey the Master. He was correct: It was a measure of destruction. But his decision to follow Jesus would have produced far more than holding onto his riches could produce.

This is exactly the issue a turnaround pastor faces, both internally and externally.

I don't think Jesus enjoyed telling this man that in order to be fully obedient, he needed to give up his wealth, but it was Jesus' love for the man that compelled Jesus to tell him the truth. We forget that Jesus endured at that moment both the pain of rejection as well as the knowledge that this man was making a decision that he would come to regret.

It is a very painful thought, and one that must be handled delicately. Jesus will ask you to bring pain into the life of your church so they can come to a place of experiencing genuine life again. Jesus will use you to destroy what is destroying your church.

You must make decisions carefully, lovingly, and sometimes tenaciously, but you will have to make these leadership decisions. If you don't, no one else will, and the default action of no decision will be a decision in and of itself.

These decisions boil down to two primary arenas: internal decisions and external decisions. Internal decisions will always precede external ones. Let me illustrate.

I knew that we needed to update our worship space. Our pews were delaminating and needed to be replaced. I knew that replacing the pews with chairs would help us create the atmosphere and culture we needed, and they were also less expensive.

I also knew that as soon as we replaced the pews, the change to our worship space would be so significant that it would disturb some of the people, but it was the right decision. So I brought up this idea in a council meeting. After some discussion, we moved on it, and I announced it to the church. Within a few weeks we had sold the pews and were setting up the chairs.

I am not exaggerating when I tell you that members of the church came to the sanctuary and stood and cried as the pews were carried out, while other members put their arms around them and comforted them. Their backs were to me, but I saw it happen. I knew I dared not intervene or again try to explain our decision. I was the bad guy. I was responsible for their pain. I had brought a level of destruction.

I knew all this was going to happen: the physical and emotional responses, the internal decision regarding the change, and the external decision to carry it out, but it didn't stop there.

As I saw the members weeping over the pews being removed, I wanted to comfort them and explain. I wanted to help and heal, and of course I felt that way—I'm a pastor. But my presence at that moment would only bring more pain, so I left, unseen.

Even though this was a relatively minor decision, some of the members felt like I'd taken their church away by changing this one small piece. While it was a small piece in my mind, it was huge to them. It took emotional energy to see their responses and how this decision had affected them. It wasn't a huge amount of emotional energy—most decisions you will make won't demand a huge amount of emotional energy, but the sheer volume of decisions you'll need to make can drain you and wear you down.

Another critical area you will need to review is how decisions are made in your leadership community. Your leadership community will have to shift for two reasons:

1. It is the current leadership paradigm that has produced these issues in the church, or at the very least, has not been able to stop the decline. You will see your leadership community change as you are able to see new leaders gain positions on your policy-making board, leaders who share your vision.

2. Your personal leadership influence must increase before you will have the platform to initiate decisions and lead the critical changes necessary in the future.

As a result, antagonists will surface in your leadership community, because they will see it as their duty to stop you and protect their church from the changes you are bringing. In their opinion, you are destroying their church, and to some degree they are right.

So how will you deal with these resisters?

Antagonists create tension to gain power, but they often believe they are confronting or resisting you to save their church. You are considered the real threat because you are now "changing everything."

What may surprise you is that many of these antagonists and resisters, who will become known in your third, fourth, or fifth years, will start out as your friends in the first few years. They will have had hopes that they could influence you not to make these changes, not to "destroy" their church. They will like things the way they are, even though they may say differently, and you are a threat.

The following definition and list of tips on dealing with antagonists is from Kenneth Haugk's book *Antagonists in the Church*. It has been a great help to me; I think I read his book four times during this phase.

DEFINING ANTAGONISM

Antagonism is not the same as healthy conflict, nor is it mere criticism. Antagonists are individuals who, on the basis of non-substantive evidence:

1. Go out of their way to make insatiable demands.

2. Attack the person or performance of others.

3. Attacks are selfish in nature.

4. Tear down rather than building up.

5. Frequently direct attacks against leadership.

10 TIPS FOR DEALING WITH ANTAGONISTS

1. Don't deal with an antagonist alone.

2. Be willing to live with them if you can and if your church can.

3. Wait for the antagonist to fully manifest himself or herself before dealing with them.

4. Get your facts documented and supported.

5. Make sure you are above reproach.

6. Watch your words and how you communicate (face-to-face, phone, email, etc.). Your words will be repeated.

7. When appropriate, bring other leaders into the mix.

8. Be prepared for criticism. It will happen if you do the right thing, the wrong thing, or nothing at all, so do the right thing.

9. Act decisively and confidently.

10. Lead clearly and courageously after a confrontation.

As you initiate significant change through internal and external decisions, there are personal and public price tags and a significant emotional output. It is very possible to experience levels of depression during this phase. Don't be afraid to get some help from a professional counselor. I did.

You are now in the most stressful period of the turnaround process because it will appear that you are destroying more than you are producing. You know the changes you are making will produce good fruit, but you don't know how long it will take. That is the challenge of the destruction phase: the destruction is immediate, but the positive results take time. You must stay the course during this season. It is simply hard work.

Now you can begin to see how the three phases at the bottom of the curve are the highest-risk area. During this time, you must make critical decisions carefully. During this phase, you are probably a threat to stakeholders in your church who are willing to fight to keep the *status quo*. It is a season of conflict, but it is only a season. Stick with it and don't quit. The best is yet to come.

During phases four, five, and six, you still run the risk of being misunderstood and having your motives questioned. But God will eventually give you leaders who will support the vision Jesus has given you for your church. This doesn't mean they will agree with you on everything. They will be honest, which can be painful, but they will be supportive. They will not see you as the problem but will stand with you to conquer the problems.

DESTRUCTION REFLECTION QUESTIONS

1. Describe your leadership community, both board members and those with influence in your church. Which leaders are supportive, and which see you as a possible threat?

2. How is Jesus asking you to respond to each one?

3. Do you have a clear idea of what needs to be "destroyed" in your church so that something greater can rise? List those things.

4. What are the objections to these changes?

5. Do you have any antagonists in your leadership community? If the answer is yes, do other leaders also concur with you? If you do have antagonists in your leadership community, and other leaders concur with you, what decision do you need to make before the church can move forward?

6. On a scale of 1–10, with 10 being *strong*, what number would you give your emotional health? What is contributing to your loss of emotional energy? If you rated yourself below six, what steps can you take to strengthen your emotional health?

7. What will you focus your prayers on during this fourth phase? List the areas you will regularly cover in prayer.

8. List out any Scriptures Jesus has put in your heart to strengthen your leadership during this fourth phase of the turnaround.

◄ TURNAROUND PHASE 5 ►
CONSTRUCTION

CONGRATULATIONS! If you are in phase five, you are a rare leader. Many turnaround pastors quit during the earlier phases and may even leave the ministry completely. You are to be commended. You have endured, survived, and lived through experiences with antagonists and resisters, and now you are ready to build.

It is impossible to pinpoint on a calendar when one phase stops and the next one begins, but phase five means you are probably four to eight years in as the turnaround pastor at this church. There are some indicators that will help you determine you are in phase five and ready for some ministry construction.

As a result of getting through phase four, you have earned the right to lead and be heard by other leaders. Your ideas have a deeper level of traction to them, and you sense you are having an impact and changing the longstanding culture in your church. Resistance is noticeably lower. This doesn't mean your ideas are always accepted or even right, but it does mean you are leading at a higher level than ever before.

You have more of the right people in the right places. Your staff and policy-making board may not be perfect, but it is noticeably better and more unified than ever before. Chances are you still have a few resisters lurking in the bushes, but don't be afraid—you will always have resisters. They are your most dependable ministry companions.

It also means you have worked pretty hard for the last four to eight years to get here. My guess is that you are tired, your spouse is tired, and maybe even your kids are tired. You probably feel emotionally spent, but you will recover with rest and time.

It was at the beginning of phase five, in 2003, that I took my first sabbatical. My sabbatical was short, but it was a meaningful time for me. I had been serving for eight years, so being able to get away from the pressures of ministry to think, pray, and rest at a deeper level was a genuine tonic. I credit this time away with being able to continue leading our church forward.

You may not be able to take a sabbatical or get away. That is completely understandable. I didn't think I could get away either, but my elders were receptive to the idea. That was a clear signal to me that our leadership community had experienced a cultural change. I was no longer considered by any of our elders to be a threat to the church. Their concern for my well-being was as healing as was their decision to grant the sabbatical.

I suggest you consider preparing the leaders on your board or council for a sabbatical, if you believe you need one. It's probably time for you to consider it. Sabbaticals at our church have been so helpful that we have written them into the policy manual for all pastoral staff who serve seven years.

If you can't get away for a sabbatical, consider a self-imposed sabbatical where you stay home, but with reduced duties. Authors Greg Asimakoupoulos and John Maxwell have written a helpful book called *The Time Crunch*. This book has a chapter in it called "Sabbatical in the Office," where Greg outlines a helpful plan to get the needed rest while staying on the job.

It is important to get rest, both physically and emotionally, because you are about to enter one of the most exciting yet taxing seasons of your leadership. Building and constructing ministry at your church will help produce a new day, and you've worked hard to get here. But building ministry will also call out further resistance, both spiritual resistance and resistance from people. Additionally, what you start out to build in terms of ministry is not what you will end up with. However, that will be okay too. Jesus has His hand in this venture.

By constructing ministry, I mean you become a cultural architect. You will be used by Jesus to shape the future of your church for years, possibly decades to come. Paul the Apostle shared the concept of building the church:

*By the grace God has given me, I laid a foundation as a wise builder, and someone else is building on it. But **each one should build** with care. For no one can lay any foundation other than the one already laid, which is Jesus Christ.*
I Corinthians 3:10–11 (emphasis mine)

Paul used the construction metaphor as he illustrated that we each build with care. There is only one foundation, and that foundation is Christ, but each one of us will build differently upon it. You are a builder, and you must see yourself as a builder. But your building materials are not brick and wood. You build with concepts, vision, strategies, and people, and this building process is more fragile and time-consuming than any other kind.

Many pastors think they can begin to construct ministry immediately upon arriving at a new church. Sometimes that is true, but it is rarely so for a turnaround pastor. Instead, you must first show the church you are trustworthy and are going to stick with this assignment. That takes a while, so be patient.

I'd like to suggest that there are six levels that you will need to build on as you lead a turnaround in your church. These levels will help create a new day for your church, since you are now at the bottom of the curve in the turnaround process. These levels are more than just stages or projects. They are ideas and values that must permeate your church's culture. These six levels of building can be seen as a leadership pyramid, as illustrated in the image below.

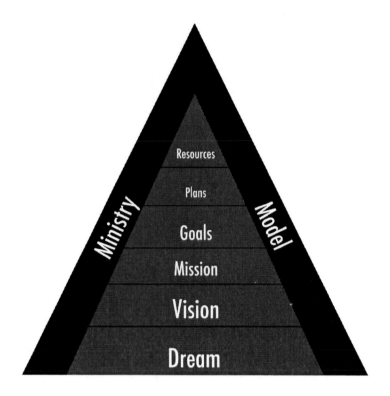

LEVEL 1: YOUR DREAM

This is the internal and very personal level of building. Let's briefly go back to when God called you into the ministry and re-explore the dream He put in your heart.

God puts dreams into the hearts of men and women, but time and people can chip away at those dreams until very little of the original dream is left. From time to time, we need to stop and reflect on the dream in our heart that propels us forward in the mission.

Abraham is an excellent example of this. God gave Abraham the dream of being the father of a great nation, but he had no children. So God gave Abraham a daily illustration to remind Him, so his dream would not die.

> *I will make your descendants as numerous as the stars in the sky.*
> *Genesis 26:4*

For many years in Abraham's life, there was very little evidence that his dream would be fulfilled. Yet every night when he went to bed, he looked up, saw the stars, and was reminded of God's dream in his heart. He chose to hold on to that dream, but that must have been difficult. Year after year, for decades, there was no baby, yet he chose to believe.

God has a way of reminding us about His dream in our heart, but it is our choice to hold on to it, or let it go. There is a lot of pressure to stop believing that God is at work when we have no tangible evidence in front of us. But believing God, despite the current evidence, both pleases God and brings the turnaround.

I had to go back to the dream in my heart of leading a prevailing church again and again. Since I was an 18-year-old boy this was the dream in my heart. I had been sidetracked in my previous church, and it looked like it would never happen in this church. But God kept saying to me, "Don't stop believing. Hold on to the dream."

Every turnaround pastor must have an internal, personal turnaround before they see an external turnaround in their church. You have to believe not only that a turnaround can happen but that God wants it to happen and He wants you to lead it. There can be massive pressure on you to quit leading your turnaround because it is taking so long. Don't do it. Choose to stay and persevere. Hold on to the dream of God in your heart.

Throughout your life, you will never move very far from your dream, so make sure you are clear about what it is. And just like Abraham, your dream will impact others. As you hold on to the dream of God in your heart, your marriage, your family, and your church will be significantly impacted by your faith. Hold on to your dream.

CONSTRUCTION: DREAM REFLECTION QUESTIONS

1. What was the dream that God put in your heart when He called you to ministry? What did you see yourself doing as a pastor as your career developed?

2. How is your current reality different than what you dreamed? What has happened to sidetrack or derail your dream?

3. Are you able to hold on to God's dream in your heart? How does your dream help you work with God to build His church? How will your dream impact others? Whom will it impact?

LEVEL 2: MISSION

We've already discussed the development of a mission statement. Your church's mission statement must reflect the dream of God in your heart because you are the champion of the vision. You are not the only carrier—and in fact, you want many people to help carry this mission—but you are the leader. Never surrender the leadership of carrying the mission forward.

Now that you have a mission statement, you need to build mission into the culture of your church. Teaching on mission, devoting time and money to mission, and deploying people into the mission does this. You will know that the mission is gaining traction when you hear your own words regarding mission coming back to you from your congregation.

Your church's mission will be worked out practically in the remaining levels, but you must take the lead for building mission into your church's culture.

CONSTRUCTION: MISSION REFLECTION QUESTIONS

1. In what ways do you use your mission statement in your church on a weekly basis?

2. How is your church's mission reflected in your annual budget, that is, what percentage of the budget supports the mission of your church, and how is it used?

3. Randomly survey your church one Sunday. Ask them to write down the mission of your church. What percentage got it right? If it is less than 25 percent, you don't yet have the traction you need to adjust culture based on the mission. What can you do to increase mission buy-in?

LEVEL 3: VISION

When you begin to cast vision, it must be public right from the start. It is not like the dream, which is internal and often private. Vision is public and is totally future-oriented. Vision is faith writing history in advance, linking with God to see that better day come into being. Vision is the natural extension of doing the mission; that's why your church's mission supports its vision, not the other way around.

I don't think you need a written vision statement as much as you need to be able to cast vision specifically for people to see it. Vision carries a clarifying component to it. It allows people to see what you see and then get involved. We make vision stick by revisiting it often. Vision answers the question, "What can we become?" and as a turnaround pastor, you must build upon that.

CONSTRUCTION: VISION REFLECTION QUESTIONS

1. If your church lived up to God's expectations in the next three years, what do you think would be different? Write out at least five specific changes you would expect to see.

2. Vision is a powerful building component, and it will excite people. But that energy will only remain if they are able to help build as well. How will the vision of your church's preferred future encourage the involvement of people? Write at least five ways you see people living out this vision in the future.

3. In a survey, ask your church this question, "If our church lived up to God's expectations, how would we be different in the next three years?" How do their answers compare to yours?

LEVEL 4: GOALS

The well-known saying "Goals are dreams with deadlines" bears repeating here. Goals move you forward and allow for the involvement of many people. You build culture in your church through goals. These goals focus on specific projects that will move the mission forward.

Good goals are public, both in development and deployment. This means that goals are developed through a team. As a turnaround pastor, you will lead the process, but everyone must own the final results.

The goal-setting acronym SMART is applicable here, because only smart goals move you forward. SMART is an acronym used often in leadership material, and it first appeared in *Management Review* magazine in 1981.

Specific: Are your goals clear enough that you know when they have been accomplished?

Measurable: Are your goals measurable? You cannot manage what you cannot measure.

Attainable: Are your goals just a little out of your reach so faith is required to reach them, but not so far out of reach that these goals are presumptuous?

Realistic: A smart goal takes into consideration what you can do. Author and pastor Nelson Searcy says, "We overestimate what we can accomplish in a year and underestimate what we can accomplish in five years."

Timely: When will this happen? Have you set reasonable deadlines?

Take a few minutes and reflect on how some well-stated, fully embraced goals for your church could help you lead a turnaround. For us, we have connected setting our goals to an annual Vision Sunday each fall. We start talking about these goals with the leadership team in the summer, and it builds excitement all summer long. Our church has now come to expect big goals each fall. Goals help us build both momentum and focus.

CONSTRUCTION: GOALS REFLECTION QUESTIONS

1. What other leaders in your church could you talk with about goals?

2. What are five specific goals that will move you forward in your mission?

LEVEL 5: PLANS

Plans are blueprints for goals. You can have all the goals you want, but until you have specific plans in place, you will see nothing accomplished.

Some leaders resist planning and say, "If God wants it to happen, then He'll just make it happen." That is true: God can make happen whatever He wants. But God Himself is a planner. I fully believe He wants me to plan as well.

Look at these Scriptures, which tell us the importance of planning.

We are warned not to plan by ourselves.
Plans fail for lack of counsel, but with many advisers they succeed.
Proverbs 15:22

Planning is a key to success.
Commit to the LORD whatever you do, and your plans will succeed.
Proverbs 16:3

Planning happens in our heart.
In his heart a man plans his course, but the LORD determines his steps.
Proverbs 16:9

Our planning connects with God's purpose.
Many are the plans in a man's heart, but it is the LORD's purpose that prevails.
Proverbs 19:21

CONSTRUCTION: PLANS REFLECTION QUESTION

Now it's time to take a look at developing some plans based on the goals you've previously set for your church. Take a look at the five specific goals you have listed previously. Make plans to help accomplish each of those goals, and write out your plans for each goal.

LEVEL 6: RESOURCES

What resources do you have? Probably more than you think. Resources tend to center around four areas: time, money, people, and space. How can we use them to move us forward or backward?

I have intentionally put resources at the top of the pyramid, because people, both leaders and followers, tend to think in limited terms. We tend to set goals based on limited resources instead of setting goals based on the mission and trusting God for the resources.

Resources are not the foundation of ministry; they are the tools of ministry. It is God's dream living in you that is the foundation of ministry. Our resources never limit God, but we do limit God by our faith. If our faith is based on limited resources, then we have limited faith. Look at this story from Jesus' ministry in Matthew 14:15–18:

> *As evening approached, the disciples came to him and said, "This is a remote place, and it's already getting late. Send the crowds away, so they can go to the villages and buy themselves some food." Jesus replied, "They do not need to go away. You give them something to eat." "We have here only five loaves of bread and two fish," they answered. "Bring them here to me," he said.*

Jesus will always ask us to do something beyond our ability and beyond our resources. Then Jesus will ask us to give Him what we have, and He will multiply it for kingdom use.

As you work through this construction pyramid, try to divert any comments about resources until the very last step. Any conversations about money, space, time, or people need to be dealt with after you've talked about what God wants you to accomplish in your church. After all, if you can reach these goals yourselves, you really don't need God at all, and that is a bad place to be as a church. As a turnaround pastor, you'll discover that God will always give you assignments that are bigger than what you can do alone.

Now it is time to ask how you will deploy your resources to reach your God-given goals. Again, don't do this alone, but as a team. When you are dealing with your resources, instead of asking, "How much do we have to work with?" ask, "How much do we need to accomplish what God wants?" God is the one who has promised to meet our needs.

I hope by now you can see that the construction phase of a turnaround church is built on the dream of God in your heart. That dream supports the mission of God that is assigned to your church. That mission leads you toward the vision of a preferred future. That vision is accomplished through specific goals and clear plans, which are fueled by God's resources. Now you are building!

INSIGHT FROM LEADERS

18 months ago I assumed the lead role with an established 80-year-old congregation. At its height it had been over 1,000 in average Sunday morning attendance. By 2005 that was down to 450 and when I assumed the leadership it was well below 100.

While the potential for our church is amazing, we were still less than 100 people with over $2.6 million of debt. We needed help! That's why I joined the Turnaround Church Coaching Network. The truth is that Don Ross and this coaching network has been the most consistent outside help we have received in our effort to turn our church around.

On Easter of 2013 we broke the 100 mark and in June of that same year we were running 130. Honestly the process is hard work and humbling but Jesus' Church is worth it.

Paul Owen
Lead Pastor, Neighborhood Church
Tualatin, OR

◄ TURNAROUND PHASES 6 AND 7 ►
DECONSTRUCTION AND
RECONSTRUCTION

ADRIAN EXPLAINED, "DON, WE HAD TO TEAR IT ALL OUT, every stick of oak. It was a beautiful hardwood floor too, but it wasn't going to work."

I'd hired Adrian to do some work on our house, and as he was estimating the work, he told me about an expensive job that had needed to be redone. He had laid a hardwood floor at a home in a Seattle suburb, and the architect had miscalculated the settling of the foundation. This settling had created a rise in the floor, and it had needed to be repaired. This meant the new oak floor with a beautiful Swedish finish had to be ripped out.

I asked him, "Didn't it bother you that you'd put in all that work only to tear it out?"

He replied, "Of course it did, but the alternative was worse. Every job I do is a living advertisement for my business. I only get work through referrals, so allowing a mediocre job to remain will only tell people I am a mediocre workman. I don't need that kind of advertisement. In this business, there is no such thing as *good enough* or *second best*. It must always be my best. These floors will last 100 years, and that is a long time to live with a mistake that could be corrected."

That is the exact thinking that every turnaround pastor must have in phase six, Deconstruction. You may think that everything you've spent the first few years building will last, but at some point you'll need to deconstruct some of what you've constructed. The alternative is to leave ineffective ministry in place, and that will only slow your progress down.

You'll also notice that phases six and seven are more directly connected: anytime you deconstruct, you'll need to reconstruct as a part of that decision. It is not enough to stop doing something; you'll also need to start doing something in its place.

Again, moving through these phases is more art than science, and you will find yourself moving both forward and backward at times in the process. You can also be in more than one phase in different areas of your church at the same time. The key is to be aware of the concepts that define each phase, so you can keep moving forward.

In the diagram of the turnaround phases (page 130), you'll notice that this phase is still in the high-tension zone. That's because any change, even change for the better, raises the tension in your church, and deconstruction raises the tension higher and faster than the original change.

If you worked for six months to get your leaders onboard for a particular change, and they now realize another change must replace the first one, you're going to get pushback.

Here's an example: You've worked hard to add another service, and you successfully launched that additional service last year. Now you realize your real bottleneck to growth is your parking, and the only way to keep growing is to add yet another service.

Your room can seat 400 people, but your parking lot can only support about 125 cars. At a ratio of one car to two people, which is pretty common in our society, you can only support a service of 250 people, and that may be stretching it because your parking capacity will begin to appear full at about 70 percent. To add even more pain, 25 percent of the 250 are children. This means you only have about 160–175 adults in your worship area that can seat 400.

You've used a lot of influence constructing a new service schedule to accommodate a second service, and you've seen your church grow as a result. Now you realize that to keep growing, you must deconstruct this service schedule and reconstruct another one, but this current service schedule still feels new to most people.

You know even if you explain this change well and get your leaders to buy into yet another change, it will still raise the tension in your church's community. But the alternative is to do nothing and lose that precious commodity called momentum. So you bite the bullet and begin the process of making yet one more change.

There are three reasons to consider deconstruction combined with reconstruction:

1. The constructed ministry never worked in the first place: If you put something in place and it is not accomplishing the goal, don't keep it going just because you want to avoid the pain of yet another change. If something you've constructed doesn't work, everyone already knows it's not working. Admit it and move on.

2. The constructed ministry worked, but now you've outgrown it: If something you put in place is successful, chances are you will outgrow it. For years in our Sunday services, we had a coffee break right after worship to greet new people and develop relationships. It worked great for a while, but eventually we had so many people it just took too long to get everyone back to continue the service. We had to deconstruct this in order to keep growing.

3. The constructed ministry can be replaced with a more effective one: Sometimes a particular ministry aspect worked well. But a church is dynamic, so what once worked must now be changed. For instance, we used to always receive our offering in the middle of the service. As we grew in our understanding of systems, we began using our communication card as a part of our sermons, asking everyone to complete one as a response to the teaching. This required moving the offering to the end of the service so people could turn in their responses. Our offerings at the end of the service have dramatically increased the people's response to the teachings.

Deconstruction is the courageous removal of systems and practices that do not fit or work. Some of you may be thinking, "Well, if you really heard from God, you'd get it right the first time." But the truth is, practices and systems have a shelf life to them, and as wise leaders, we need to be ready to make the needed adjustment to keep pursuing the mission.

You'll also notice in the diagram of the turnaround phases, that the deconstruction phase is between the construction and reconstruction phases. This means these three are linked in process, so every constructed thing may have to be deconstructed so it can be reconstructed.

Let me give you a couple of painful, but productive examples of this process. The first one is our small groups ministry. We launched our small groups three different times before they gained traction.

Before moving to Seattle, I was a part of Christ the King (CTK) in Bellingham, Washington. I had helped plant this church in the 1980s and then left to pastor my first church. I returned to CTK for a while to serve as executive pastor. They had an outstanding small group ministry, which I later tried to duplicate in Creekside for about two years. I gave it a noble effort, but it didn't work—we never had more than eight groups at any one time.

It was a dismal failure. And after two years of effort, not only did I have to deconstruct this ministry, I had to wait a season before starting small groups again. The second time, I tried a cell group model where every group had to discuss the sermon each week. They were to grow and multiply into a new group each year. But resistance was high; no one wanted to do that. Again, my effort failed, and again I had to wait and let the culture purge itself of the memory of yet another failure before trying again.

Then about three years ago, we discovered Nelson Searcy's book *Activate*, and we immediately began to put that system into practice. It allowed the freedom necessary to help people connect, and we grew in one year from 8 small groups to 32 small groups. Now we offer small groups in three semesters each year. We only promote groups three months during the whole year, yet we regularly have over 40 small groups meeting now. We still need more small groups, but we have regular traction in our groups. This is a huge success.

Part of the success was finding the ministry with the right fit, and part of the success was that our culture had shifted enough so we had higher acceptance than resistance. Honestly, I can't tell you which came first, but both were important.

Any pain involved in deconstructing ministry has long been forgotten as we enjoy the success of seeing effective ministry take place. I am well aware that growth may produce a season of deconstruction in the future, but for now, we're enjoying this season.

Another area we had to deconstruct was our ministry model, and again it took three attempts to get this right. I am amazed that our congregation let me practice on them like this, but they did. I will be ever grateful for the blessed flexibility of Creekside Church.

At first, I resisted the idea of a ministry model, but I gradually came to accept the value of such a tool. I'll tell you more on that subject later, but for now it is enough to say that a ministry model is an example of how your church works out its mission. It is a picture of how your church does ministry, and it helps people discover where they fit in.

Our first effort at a ministry model was to try and copy what I had learned from CTK in Bellingham, but it just didn't work in Seattle. Our attempt at copying their ministry model died during our first small group failure.

I started looking for someone else to copy, and since Rick Warren's book *The Purpose Driven Church* was popular, I copied that model. I tried to make our church look like a baseball diamond and get everyone on board with this plan. Again, it failed, and I could feel that I was losing influence.

I was discouraged. One night my wife and I were talking, and Brenda said, "I know you're looking for a model to follow, but copying what someone else has done probably isn't going to work. God is creative. I think a ministry model has to come out of your heart."

I replied, "You're probably right, but I don't think I have time to craft this out on my own. Honestly, I'm looking for a shortcut to help us get some traction. Why should I reinvent the wheel?"

As I look back, the fastest way to develop a solid ministry model would have been to take some time with Jesus to read, pray, think, and write, but I was looking for a quick turnaround. I now know there is no such thing. Jesus is not interested in *quick* as much as He is interested in *right*. As a leader, I felt like I was always weighing the benefits between short-term (quick) and long-term (right). But with Jesus, the long term is the only lens He looks through when it comes to building ministry. Jesus doesn't seem as interested in a quick turnaround as much as a healthy turnaround.

And with that I was on to the next failure. Andy Stanley came along with his *environments*, and I bought into it big-time. Andy identified his church like a house, with a foyer, a living room, and finally the kitchen, which represented small groups where people really connected with one another. I was so taken with this that I flew to Atlanta, went to yet another seminar, and came home with yet another plan. I deconstructed the baseball diamond and reconstructed the ministry house.

We started opening our services by welcoming everyone to our "front room," and we encouraged them to move to the kitchen to get to know one another and make friends. Now, I love Andy, and he has inspired me greatly. But this didn't work any better than anything else I had tried. It was deconstructed after about 18 months of effort, and this time I had nothing to put in its place.

Inside my head, I kept hearing Brenda's words, "This is going to come out of your heart." In the same way that God's dream in your heart is the foundation of the ministry He wants to do through you, a ministry model will come from your heart as well.

I had almost given up on seeing a ministry model constructed. It seemed like I had done more deconstructing than constructing. I began to think that having a ministry model just wasn't necessary. Jesus didn't have one, and neither did Paul (or did they?). I confided in a friend that I thought just having a working mission statement was enough, but in my heart I knew different.

Then one day I was sitting in my office, praying and thinking about this, and I looked up at a clock made from a ship's wheel. It had six handles on it, and I saw our six purposes from Acts 2:42–47:

They devoted themselves to the apostles' teaching [Spiritual Growth] and to the fellowship, to the breaking of bread and to prayer. Everyone was filled with awe, and many wonders and miraculous signs were done by the apostles. All the believers were together and had everything in common. Selling their possessions and goods, they gave to anyone as he had need [Ministry, Serving]. Every day they continued to meet together in the temple courts. They broke bread in their homes and ate together with glad and sincere hearts [Community], praising God [Worship] and enjoying the favor of all the people. And the Lord added to their number daily those who were being saved [Outreach].

Creekside Ministry Model

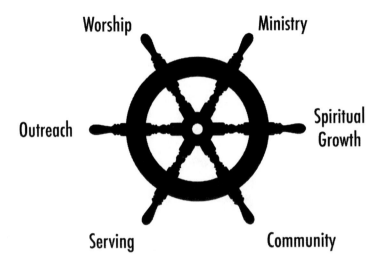

Worship   Ministry

Outreach   Spiritual
                                            Growth

Serving   Community

I love being on a boat, and the whole idea that our ministry model was attached to such an image reached my heart. I felt like Jesus was saying, "Let's do this together."

Each of the six purposes was supported from Scripture, and it provided a balanced way of doing ministry. Now we have since added three strategies that each support two purposes. It has become a very simple way of describing how our church works, and people get it. It is a map to help people understand where they fit.

Creekside Strategies

Sunday Gatherings

Servant Outreach

Groups

We ask the people of Creekside Church to do three things, all of which support the purposes of our church: be in a worship service regularly, be in a community group, and serve.

These strategies support the purposes, which in turn support the mission. This ministry model has gained tremendous traction, and Jesus has used it wonderfully. Every other ministry model felt like I was trying to force a square peg into a round hole. It just didn't work. Like David in the Old Testament, I was trying to wear someone else's battle gear, but I had to find my own weapons.

If you have adopted Andy Stanley's ministry model or Rick Warren's ministry model, that's great. I hope it is working well for you. All I'm saying is that I knew in my heart Jesus wanted something for us that came from my heart, and I was resisting His prompting, trying to short-cut and accelerate the turnaround process. That actually only slowed the process down. I learned that slow, effective obedience accomplishes Godly goals faster than quick, ineffective disobedience.

A word of warning: During this phase, there will be high emotional output, by both the pastor and the congregation. All change requires additional emotional output, even positive change.

This intense season of change can be very frustrating, which in turn increases the possibility of mistakes. This is a time to watch what you say even more than usual. As the turnaround pastor, you are leading in uncharted waters, so choose your words carefully, even more so than you normally would. Being a steady, focused leader will allow Jesus to build confidence in your people.

I am reminded of a high season of change during Israel's history. Moses was gone, Joshua was taking over, and he was nervous. Four times in the first chapter of Joshua, he is told to "be strong." Choosing to be strong is a personal choice for any leader. Joshua apparently wasn't feeling strong, so God was encouraging him.

God helped Joshua, and He will help you. As Joshua walked with God, the people of Israel saw God working through their leader, which is what your people really want to see in you.

> *Then they answered Joshua, "Whatever you have commanded us we will do, and wherever you send us we will go. Just as we fully obeyed Moses, so we will obey you. Only may the Lord your God be with you as he was with Moses."*
> *Joshua 1:16–17*

Your people want to know that you are walking with God. They know instinctively that you don't have all the answers, and they are okay with that. But they need to know that you are in touch with Jesus, because He does have the answers.

Even Joshua had to do a few things over. He had to attack the city of Ai twice because he didn't ask the counsel of the Lord. The people still followed him, and they will follow you too. If you genuinely want to do the right thing, and you are honestly seeking the Lord, you will see your church begin to turn in the right direction.

DECONSTRUCTION AND RECONSTRUCTION REFLECTION QUESTIONS

1. List every program, ministry, and operation of your church in every area (e.g., facilities, finances, children, youth, adult, groups, worship, services, etc.).

2. Now rate the items on that list, rating each ministry on a scale of 1–10, with 10 being *highly effective* and 1 being *entirely ineffective*.

3. List the top three most ineffective ministries, and write out why you believe they need to be deconstructed and what needs to be reconstructed in their place.

4. What will you focus your prayers on during these phases? List the areas you will regularly cover in prayer.

5. List out any Scriptures Jesus has put in your heart to strengthen your leadership during these phases of the turnaround.

◄ TURNAROUND PHASES 8 AND 9 ►
PRODUCTION AND REPRODUCTION

THE NEXT TWO PHASES ARE ROCKET RIDES compared to the rest. They are both strange and wonderful, and you'll have to remind yourself from time to time what you went through to get here.

After working so hard for so long with minimal results, phase eight will be the opposite. You will experience increasing results with what you will now consider minimal effort. Strange. And wonderful.

Enjoy this season. Very few pastors and churches get here; so take time to reflect on how far you've come. Produce graphs that show your upward trends in giving and attendance, but don't lose sight of the mission your church has been assigned.

You are not out of danger, and in fact, you will never be out of danger as a church. Don't ever think you can take your ease or back off from leading as a turnaround pastor. You are now seeing some wonderful results. Morale is high, new people are coming to Christ, and your church is growing. But you need to keep leading and pressing the mission forward, or your church will slip backward.

Phase eight takes some time to get used to, since you have been in survival mode for so long and moving into a thriving mode seems very strange. Here are some indicators that you are moving into phase eight:

Momentum and morale: There is a clear sense that the church is moving forward. Your worship services seem effective, and people are bringing their friends. You feel like your words are making a difference when you preach.

Not only are your attendance numbers trending upward but, after you've been in phase eight awhile, there are more and more people you don't know in your church. You have to be okay with this. The focus needs to be that everyone knows someone, not that everyone knows you.

Finances: After years of trending downward, you have leveled off, and now you are trending upward in your church finances. You sense it may be time to hire staff, renovate your facilities, or lead a missions project. You are a little nervous because you are not convinced that your church's giving will continue to increase. It's very understandable to feel this way, so be cautious—but not to the point of stunting your growth or momentum. It is important to step out in faith during this time. God is not causing you and your church to prosper so you can relax or hoard resources. Press the mission forward.

Ministry: During this phase you see your ministries prosper and grow. New ministries begin to sprout, and other people with vision stand alongside you. It can become easy to lose focus with more going on, so stay close to your mission. Your church is moving from being a turn-around church to a vibrant church. You are not quite there yet, but you are closer than ever before. Both you and the congregation can sense this good change.

Culture: People are talking less and less about the good old days, and you feel a shift take place in the atmosphere of your church. After worship services you see people talking in groups with each other, instead of heading quickly for the door. New people tell you they feel welcome, and it's not just because you publicly welcome them from the stage. New people now bring other new people with them to worship services. New friendships and relationships develop, and things in general seem to be thriving.

This is not to say that you don't have an occasional challenge. People still leave your church and issues flare up, but the trend is now clearly toward solid spiritual health for your church.

Leadership: Your leadership has come into a new space, and you no longer feel like you are living in a ministry minefield. There is a feeling that you could actually continue to lead this church. There are still problems to deal with, but the personal attacks are rare; you are leading a leadership community that you know is supportive. These advocates each believe in the mission and trust you, and they are doing their part to move it forward as well.

The danger in phase eight is that you will likely feel you have arrived and may slack off in pressing the mission. The resisters are rare, and resources are on the rise. You are, perhaps, preaching to more people than ever before, and the church is now beginning to surge.

But you are now in danger of a new enemy. Your new enemy is success. Since you now have more, you will need to be willing to risk more to keep moving forward in the mission.

The old danger was seeing the church go out of business, so in a sense, you had nothing to lose by taking risks. But now you have some success and are starting to thrive a little, so the risk is greater. The more you have, the more you can lose. This fear must be conquered, or you will never make it into phase nine and see reproduction take place.

In one sense, your church is like a young married couple that has just gotten out of debt, using both incomes. After being financially strapped for years, you are free from your huge debt load and are talking about having children.

In your heart, you'd love to have children, but you also know that in order for that to happen, your wife will need to quit her job to fulfill her dream of being a stay-at-home mom. That translates into less income and, when the baby comes, increased expenses. You are concerned that a baby could plunge you into debt again, so you put the decision off, unwilling to take the risk.

You can delay this opportunity for a while but not forever. At some point you will run out of time, and the decision will be made for you. But think of it this way: Did you work hard to get out of debt so you could spend your earnings on yourselves? Or is being out of debt part of the plan so you can have a family—so you can reproduce?

As a turnaround pastor, you have already devoted a good portion of your life to seeing a dying church come back to life again. It has been years of hard work, and many of the people who are with you now did not live through those days. It also serves no purpose to keep reminding them how hard it was.

Most of those who are with you now are here as a result of a compelling mission. If you buckle under the pressure and refuse to risk moving forward, then you are not only sacrificing the mission, you are eroding the very clarion call that first attracted many of those with you now. You may feel secure for a while, but that feeling in the pit of your stomach will not go away. You are now at the point where you will decide to lead your church into the next phase.

Phase nine is Reproduction. There are several ways to experience reproduction as a church. Continued growth is reproduction. New people are now bringing other new people. They are reproducing the life of Christ in others as they share the gospel.

But let's be honest here, that kind of reproduction is going to happen anyway, and it should. You want those in your church to each be disciple-makers, and you're going to do all you can to encourage that to happen.

The kind of reproduction I'm talking about is much riskier than this and also much more rewarding. I'm talking about giving away ministry to others, just like Jesus gave it away.

When Jesus was here on earth, He trained his disciples to do ministry. After His resurrection, Jesus remained another forty days, further training them, and then ascended into heaven. He literally gave the church away to these men. Over the next few decades, each one of those disciples scattered across the known world, spreading the gospel, and they, in turn, gave ministry away to others.

It seems like the more successful we are, the more we are called to give away. It also appears that the more successful we are, the more we struggle with giving ministry away. In some ways, the risk of continued ministry rises with our success because the more we have, the more will be asked of us. Jesus said it like this:

From everyone who has been given much, much will be demanded; and from the one who has been entrusted with much, much more will be asked.
Luke 12:48

This is purely a leadership issue. Most of your church will be very happy not to risk anything and never to move into the reproduction and multiplication of phase nine. There is a constant pull toward safety and security in all of us, but refusing to risk isn't obedient faith. It is disobedience and will lead the church back into the appearance of life only (Revelation 3:1).

In the same way that the safety of *status quo* is the mark of death to the institutionalized church, the producing church that refuses to reproduce itself will quickly lose momentum. You cannot stop moving forward in the Kingdom. You are either progressing or regressing.

I am not saying you should recklessly throw your resources away in frivolous attempts to reproduce. A wise leader will not do that. My purpose here is to address the attitude of reproduction rather than the method. My assignment here is to challenge you to keep moving forward, even in the wake of possible failures.

Most reproduction will take place through planting new churches or developing a multisite approach. God uses both. You will need to determine where Jesus is calling you. You will need to resource yourself by reading, planning, and learning from others.

In February 2012, we made our first effort at reproduction. We adopted another church, and it was going to be our first multisite campus. Prior to this, our church helped plant six other churches, fully mothering one and becoming planting partners for the other five. The church we were now adopting was a church we had helped plant some thirteen years before.

As our team prepared for the official adoption date of September 2012, we were excited to be stretching out. We had scheduled an adoption announcement service for May of 2012 and asked the founding pastor to speak. The current pastor, who would become the new campus pastor and part of our staff, was there also. This church had been running about 90 people and just needed some structure and strategy. The staff and I had good chemistry with the new campus pastor, and we were all optimistic about the results.

September came, and we were ready to reproduce and multiply. We had new banners printed, we handed out new programs the first

Sunday, and I put myself into the teaching lineup. It looked like all systems were go for a great launch, but looks were deceiving.

The wheels came off the wagon quickly over the next six weeks. The attendance dropped from 90 to 18 people, and it became clear we didn't have the critical mass to continue. We met with everyone who was part of the campus and talked it through, finally making the painful decision to pull the plug on this campus and discontinue.

In this conversation, we began to understand some expectations that we had failed to fulfill. This group of 90 had expected that being adopted by a larger church meant we would be sending people to help with serving. Some did go, but not to serve. They went because it was closer to where they lived.

As a leadership team we expected that just providing good leadership and strategy would breathe new life into this group. But that did not happen either. The final blow was coming to understand that the campus pastor, who had led this church for the last four years, was emotionally exhausted, which had not surfaced in our interviews. He needed a break to reassess and recharge.

We made the decision to continue to support this campus pastor for a few months and help him relocate to another city, where he and his family are now flourishing. We remain good friends, and he is serving in a great church, contributing to the advancement of the Kingdom.

This was our first venture at moving from production to reproduction, and it failed. During that same period of time, we were renting to an ethnic church, and that venture failed as well. Both of these situations created a desire in me to run for safety. I was done trying to move into reproduction. And all of this happened while writing this manuscript.

But Jesus would allow no retreat. About six months after closing down both of these ministries, I received a call from one of our ministry network leaders at the Northwest Ministry Network. This has been a good association for us, and I am well supported. The clear focus of this ministry network has been to train churches and pastors to reach lost people, even at the expense of some deeply held traditions. I appreciate the courage with which the leadership has moved in this direction, but the call I received was personally challenging.

Our network was focusing on a theme of multiplication, which I certainly endorsed. The basic concept was that churches need to move from simple addition to multiplication. Addition means adding people to the Kingdom one at a time. While addition is worthy, multiplication is much more effective. The New Testament church started with addition (Acts 2:47) but quickly moved into multiplication (Acts 6:7). Multiplication means not only adding new churches, but also challenging existing churches to plant new churches and even develop a multi-site approach to ministry.

This call was a request for us to consider embracing a Latino congregation as a part our own church. The pastor would eventually become a staff pastor, and this group would become a new Spanish-speaking service at Creekside Church. In my heart, I knew this was another possibility at moving toward the reproduction phase, but I was hesitant. After two failed attempts, I was not sure this one would fly either.

Simply put, I was afraid of failing. We had had some remarkable success over the last three years, seeing a growth rate of 22 percent each year, increased giving, new believers, and more small groups. I didn't want to jeopardize morale with a third failure at reproducing. As a congregation, there was still a slight sting when the topic of expansion came up.

I chose to send our executive pastor, Jason, to meet with the leadership of this Latino group. Jason is analytical, and I wanted his assessment. He had lived through the two failed reproduction attempts, and if this one were going to succeed, I needed his input and support. I am reluctant to say that I was afraid to go, but it is an honest evaluation to say that I was distancing myself from the initial input.

When Jason came back from meeting with the leaders of this group, he was enthusiastic about the opportunity. We talked through my issues of reluctance and then felt ready to take it to the elders. After some council-level discussion, we welcomed the Latino group as a part of Creek side Church.

We moved ahead, launching a Spanish service, and it has been fully embraced by our congregation. They are not renting space from us; they are part of us, and we are part of them. I will be teaching in this service monthly, since I am their pastor too.

As I look back on this venture, which is just barely out of the starting gate, I realize it could have all been crushed. When I received the call from the network leadership, I could have simply said, "No." That would have been the end of it... or would it?

Jesus has a way of prodding us to increasing levels of risk to move the Kingdom forward. My sense is that even if I had said no to this opportunity, there would have been others. In addition to embracing this Spanish service, we are moving toward new campuses in the future. We are called to reproduce ourselves, both as disciples and as local churches.

I remember being asked during a leadership training session what the fruit of an apple tree was. The obvious answer was an apple, and while true, that is not the full answer. The real fruit of an apple tree is another apple tree. The tree produces an apple, which contains seeds, which can be planted to produce another apple tree. The cycle of reproduction is not complete until another tree has been produced.

It is the same for us. We are truly disciples of Jesus when we have produced disciples who have produced disciples. We have not fully discipled anyone for Christ until they have also learned to make disciples themselves.

I believe the same is true for churches. In the same way each disciple must reproduce, each church must also reproduce itself, but as the leader, you hold the decision-making key as to whether or not that will happen.

The greatest challenge to our leadership lies in between production and reproduction, because our most powerful leadership decisions will take place here. It is in this phase that we decide either to embrace the lie of risk-free ministry and hold to *status quo*, or accept our greatest challenges yet, moving forward to reproduce and multiply.

When you have led a ministry that had no resources, and have seen that ministry grow after having resources added, it is incredibly difficult to risk again. But that is the courageous decision Jesus calls us to make. That is what it takes to move the Kingdom forward: the faith to risk again and again.

There is a popular story about putting faith into action, which is exactly what every turnaround pastor is called to do.

After being lost in the desert for days, a man came to an abandoned farm with a well and a water pump. His hopes rose. At the well, he saw a jar of water, and he knew he would be saved from dying a horrible death. But there was a note attached to the jar.

The note read:

Dear friend,

The water here is good and plentiful. The pump works well. However, it is used so little that it dries out between uses and must be primed with the water in this jar. Do not drink the water in this jar, but pour it all down the well and then begin pumping. In a short time, you will have plenty of water. Warning: you must use ALL of the water in the jar to prime the pump. Do not drink any of this water, or there will not be enough to prime it. When you are through, remember to refill this jar for the next person.

Desert Pete

The man was so thirsty he almost drank the water anyway. After all, who would know? Then he thought, *What if the person before me had not done what the note asked? I would have no hope. It worked for him.*

He picked up the jar, reluctantly poured all of its contents in, and pumped the handle. He waited, hoping expectantly. He began to hear the water coming and pumped harder. Soon he saw the fresh, clean, cool water that saved his life.

It is not an exaggeration to say that the note written on that jar saved his life. The note was true, and he believed it, acted on it, and lived.

But what if he had played it safe and had just drunk the water? He might have lived, but whoever came out of the desert after him and found the well would not have been so fortunate. They would have found an empty jar. This man's faith in Desert Pete's note saved his life and the lives of those who came behind him, although he would never know them.

Pastor, that is the story of you and me. We wrestle through decisions like this in our prayer time with Jesus, as He asks us to risk it all, to pour all the water down the pump.

Part of the issue is that we look at the potential loss before the potential gain. Take a minute and ask yourself the questions below, and reflect on your next ministry steps.

PRODUCTION AND REPRODUCTION REFLECTION QUESTIONS

1. List three to five areas of ministry where you are seeing production, that is, success. What criteria are you using to define this success?

2. What do you sense Jesus is asking you to do to move the mission forward now?

3. Where is Jesus asking you to take a risk in reproduction? What ministry decision have you been avoiding, that you are even reluctant to write down?

4. What would you do if you knew you couldn't fail and you knew you had God's promise to succeed?

INSIGHT FROM LEADERS

It was nine months ago that I was invited to an informational luncheon for the Turnaround Church Coaching Network. While I was very interested in attending, I felt it was financially out of the question. Don Ross encouraged me and helped me step past my excuses and God showed the way. I have been a pastor for over 40-years and was seeking a lot of directional answers at this time of my life.

The very first class, where we met with a small group of pastors, literally set a fire under me for what I believed God was going to do with us all He used Don to challenge us each month. Creekside Church also provided us with prayer support the duration of the TCCN. We began to march through the information and read the challenging books by insightful men of God. While the process for integrating these Biblical concepts is not done over night, still I began to realize positive results immediately, both in my church and most of all in me.

Today our church leadership team is totally committed to the steps learned at TCCN. Our church, while small, has doubled in size and the stewardship of this congregation has greatly increased. We have also been able to increase our support to missions. I could go on, but I want to simply thank the Lord for what has happened in the life of our church. I would encourage every pastor to find the time and a way to be part of the Turnaround Church Coaching Network, a step you will not regret.

Pastor Bob Smith
Pastor of Covenant Fellowship,
Poulsbo, WA

FINAL WORDS

IN THIS LAST CHAPTER. I'd like to focus on some critical issues that every turnaround pastor must face, both internally and externally. It may come across as a bit of a mixed bag, but I honestly had in my mind this thought: *If I only had one hour to coach a turnaround pastor, what are the most helpful tips I could give him or her?*

To be a turnaround pastor, Jesus must call you, but that's true for any pastor, or at least it should be. The unique role of a turnaround pastor is that you are called to reverse the decline of a dying church, and most declining or plateaued churches refuse to admit they are dying. So the very first message you communicate is not a message of hope, but a message of alarm. Hope will come later, after the church realizes they are in danger.

You are called to help raise the dead and to see a better day when no one else around can or will. You know going in that it will be a long and difficult road, yet you go anyway out of a sense of calling, not knowing how long or how difficult it will be.

You know in your heart that things must change, and you have some idea as to what those changes must be. All leaders bring change, and pastors are no different. Change is constantly on a turnaround pastor's mind because only change will bring a better day. But bringing about change is no easy job. It's hard enough to think about which changes need to be made first and how to go about making them.

UNDERSTAND THE SYSTEMIC NATURE OF YOUR CHURCH

The church is a living organism, not a club or an institution. As a result, it has a life of its own. This makes the church more systemic in nature than systematic, and every turnaround pastor needs to know this fact. You ignore this information to your own peril because this one issue can stop your leadership momentum in its tracks.

There is a lot of information on the difference between being systematic and systemic. For our purposes, we're going to keep the definitions simple. Something is *systemic* when all of the parts are interconnected to all of the other parts.

For example, your body is systemic in nature. If you smash your thumb, your whole body knows about it and reacts accordingly. If you catch a cold, your whole body deals with the infection. Your head would never say to your smashed thumb, "I'm up here, and you're down there; your pain is your problem." Your thumb and your head suffer together. They are part of the same body. This is what the Apostle Paul is referring to in I Corinthians 12:26, when he says, "If one member suffers, we all suffer."

Something that is *systematic* is more methodical. An automobile assembly line is systematic. If you have twenty machines all performing different tasks in an assembly line, and one machine goes down and needs to be replaced, the other machines don't feel the loss, or resist the change. You just repair or replace the machine and start up the assembly line again. A change in one area doesn't affect other areas.

But if there is a change in a systemic environment, each change affects every other area. It's like a child's mobile, hanging over a crib. If you touch one part of the mobile, every part moves.

Why is it critical for you to understand that your church is systemic in nature? It is critical because every change you make, or try to make, will affect every other area of your church. Each decision has far-reaching impact, well beyond what you think.

Here's an example: You believe that an 80-year-old man in your church who has served as an usher at the church door for thirty-five years needs to be replaced. He is well-loved by seasoned members and is almost a Sunday morning fixture, but he no longer hears well and simply doesn't welcome new people. After watching for several months, you decide to make a replacement. You honor him for his years of service and gently, lovingly ask if he would be willing to give up this ministry and consider a different place of service.

You now have a potential systemic problem.

You believe you've handled the situation well. You've assessed it logically and approached this brother lovingly and honorably. There really shouldn't be a problem because everyone should know why you are encouraging this decision, especially if they want the church to grow. After all, new people decide within minutes if they will return to your church again, and how they are greeted is critical to a good first impression.

What you don't know is that you just lost a key children's ministry volunteer the minute you asked this usher to make room for others to serve. This man's daughter, who served in the children's ministry, heard about this decision and was so offended that she quit. And now you have two problems to deal with—or maybe three.

You see, her husband is a key member of the board. And what you don't know is that your next board meeting will be dominated by a discussion of your uncaring attitude toward volunteers. Already this board member is calling other board members to report your decision. This all happened because you asked an ineffective, but deeply loved usher to step down and consider a different ministry.

You want to make a change that will move your church forward, but the church culture wants to keep things the same. You are dreaming of those people yet to come, welcoming and making room for them. The established members are dreaming of keeping the family together, and your decisions appear to be tearing them apart. Your appeals that such decisions need to be made for the sake of the mission fall upon deaf ears and appear uncaring and callous.

All of us have to be willing to give up our ministries at some point. Jesus gave up His earthly ministry to others, and so will we—but the tension for the pastor in communicating this truth can be difficult. It will help to know that your church is systemic and that everyone is connected, somehow, to every decision made.

There is no silver bullet for dealing with this issue. This is part of the minefield of church leadership. It may be helpful to think through a decision like this and ask yourself, "Who else will be affected by this move?" and then act accordingly. The best news I have for you on this subject is, the longer you serve your church, the more your heart is known. The better your heart is known, the less you will be misunderstood, and the fewer land mines you will trip.

LEARN HOW TO LEAD THROUGH CHANGE

So how do you bring about change and make critical decisions as a turnaround pastor? Here is a helpful model that I have used many times. It is not foolproof, and it doesn't guarantee success. But understanding this model will give you a fighting chance.

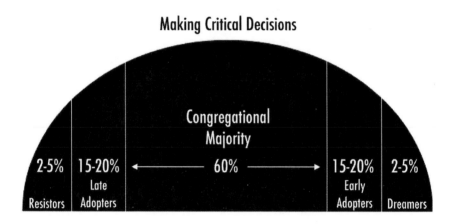

Making Critical Decisions

Congregational Majority

| 2-5% | 15-20% | ←——— 60% ———→ | 15-20% | 2-5% |
| Resistors | Late Adopters | | Early Adopters | Dreamers |

I first became aware of this model in a book called *The Pastor's Manual for Effective Ministry* by the late Win Arn. This book is a series of articles by Arn. In this one he helps us understand how a group of people, like your church, will respond to a new initiative, decision, or change.

When you propose a new idea, the Dreamers, about 2–5 percent, will be on board right away. They will have very few questions and will be fans and promoters almost immediately. All you will need to do with them is cheer them on and give them solid reasons for this decision, so they can share your logic with others.

The next group, Early Adopters, represents up to 15–20 percent of your church. They are very favorable toward your leadership and want your new initiative to work, but they have a few questions. You'll have to spend some time with these people, understand their questions, and give them solid answers. Don't be intimidated or defensive, just listen carefully and give clear responses, and they will not only be on board but they will invite others to join them.

Now let's go to the other end of the model and look at the Resisters. This represents about 2–5 percent of your church. They will disagree with virtually anything you ever come up with. They would disagree with Jesus Himself, so you don't have a chance. Be polite and compassionate with this group, but don't worry about making friends or getting them on board. It's never going to happen. If you begin conceding to their demands to win loyalty, there will be no end. Stay focused on the mission, which this change supports.

Resisters will pepper you will endless questions, which will be rooted in an attempt to stop you, or at least slow you down. This is the area where antagonists hide out, and they will try to get their friends on board and try to build resistance. Be sure you communicate with this group well. Answer their questions as best you can, but be prepared spiritually and emotionally to move forward without their support, because you will not get it.

The value of this group of Resisters is twofold: First, they will help you rethink your initiative. If you really are interested in producing a good change in your church, you have to hear from detractors as well as supporters. Detractors will point out flaws and considerations you may have overlooked. They do this to stop you, but you should use this information to strengthen your decision by addressing the flaws they point out. In fact, if what they bring up completely dismantles your idea, face the truth. Don't try and make a bad idea work just to save face. That will seriously erode your leadership influence.

Secondly, everyone else is watching how you handle the resistance. This is an opportunity for you to show you can stand strong, yet remain caring at the same time. Every time a Resister comes against you, you have a wonderful opportunity to gain influence as a leader, based on how you respond. If you listen, ask questions, and then thank them for their input, you have not only weakened their resistance, you may even convince them you really do care about them and this church.

The next group is the Late Adopters, and they will make up about 15–20 percent of your church. They will have many questions and may not support you, but if you answer their questions, they won't resist much. The Resisters either don't like you or the initiative you're putting forth, but the Late Adopters simply don't like change. Your goal with this group should be to listen to their concerns, then answer their questions, and hope for some mild support but at least no open resistance.

The final group is the roughly 60% congregational majority. This majority will follow whichever group, at either end, has the most influence. If your most influential leaders are resisters or late adopters, then you are facing an uphill challenge for sure.

But as the pastor, you hopefully have the most influential leaders as Dreamers, as well as Early Adopters. If you have given them biblical and logical reasons for your initiative, you will be able to move forward. Just be patient, and let your leadership culture work.

CAN THIS CHURCH LIVE AGAIN?

In Ezekiel 37, the prophet gives us a picture of the church you may be leading; at least it was a picture of our church.

> *The hand of the Lord was on me, and he brought me out by the Spirit of the Lord and set me in the middle of a valley; it was full of bones. He led me back and forth among them, and I saw a great many bones on the floor of the valley, bones that were very dry. He asked me, "Son of man, can these bones live?" I said, "Sovereign Lord, you alone know." Then he said to me, "Prophesy to these bones and say to them, 'Dry bones, hear the word of the Lord! This is what the Sovereign Lord says to these bones: I will make breath enter you, and you will come to life. I will attach tendons to you and make flesh come upon you and cover you with skin; I will put breath in you, and you will come to life. Then you will know that I am the Lord.'"*
> *Ezekiel 37:1–6*

In these few verses, this conversation between God and the prophet sums up the picture of a declining church. It shows what God has called a turnaround pastor to do, what God has promised He will do through you.

In many ways your church may be like a valley of dry bones. It used to be alive, but now it is not. Every bone in this valley without life is like the lifeless stories you hear about how your church used to be vibrant and alive. The huge sanctuary used to be filled, but now only a few gather. The parking lot used to be packed, but now it's mostly empty. Many of the classrooms are no longer needed, and the list can go on about how things used to be. Your church once had a great influence in the community, but now that is gone too.

God has brought you to this place, as He brought the prophet Ezekiel to the valley, and God is asking you a similar question, "Can this church live again?"

How will you answer him? If you say as Ezekiel said, "Only you know, Lord," then God will say to you what He said to Ezekiel: "Speak life to these bones."

God is asking you to do for your church what Ezekiel did for those dry bones, to give them life by speaking life to them. You are being called to see with the eyes of faith what God wants to accomplish through you and your church. You are being called by God to love these people and the ones who will come. You are being called by God to honor the memories of this church's past and cast vision for a preferred future at the same time.

But God must have a leader who will believe what He says. Your church must have a pastor who honestly believes that a better day is coming and that a God-given mission can be accomplished.

So here are two questions for you to consider:

1. Do you believe God has called you to lead this church out of death and into life, out of decline and into growth, and out of selfishness and into selflessness for the sake of the mission of God?

2. Will you hold onto this vision of life, vitality, and growth for your church for however long it takes to accomplish your assignment? Or is leading this church part of your career path and just a stepping-stone to you?

AM I THE ONE TO LEAD THIS CHURCH?

I cannot begin to tell you the number of times I asked myself the question above. There were so many times when resistance was steep, or money was tight, or people were leaving our church, and I would ask myself again. Year after year as our numbers declined while we were building a new culture, I asked myself again, "Am I the one to do this?" I wanted to quit so many times, but I found myself coming back to a simple, very encouraging thought, *I must be able to do this assignment, or Jesus would not have given it to me.*

I think Joshua may have felt this way. After being with Moses for 40 years, seeing so many miracles, and helping him turn a nation of slaves into a conquering army, Joshua must have thought as they approached the Promised Land that victory was within sight.

And suddenly Moses was dead, and Joshua was on his own as the leader. He must lead where Moses had led. The people now looked to him as they had looked to Moses. He was now responsible for the millions who made up this mobile nation. I think Joshua may have asked, "Am I really the one to lead this group?"

There is a reason why Joshua chapter 1 records God saying four times, "Be strong and courageous": I don't think Joshua necessarily felt strong and courageous. But to his credit, Joshua manned up and stepped into the leadership role God had given him. And Israel moved forward. Joshua made his mistakes, but he owned them. And they moved forward.

The people only required one thing from Joshua, and that is what your church is asking of you. This desire is summed up in Joshua 1:17, *"Only may the Lord your God be with you as he was with Moses."* Your people want to know that God is with you.

This journey you are being called to lead is not just a journey of you leading your church. It is also the deepening of a relationship between you and God. You cannot do this on your own.

You must learn about ratios, lifecycles, and phases, but more importantly, this is about trusting God to work through you. You need to know how to deal with antagonists and resisters and how to bring about change, but if these decisions are simply techniques, they will not succeed. Your heart must be in the hands of the Almighty, and believe me, the people know if God has your heart or not.

At one point in Joshua's leadership, he became confident in his own ability and did not ask counsel of the Lord (Joshua 7) when they tried to take the city of Ai. Israel was soundly defeated. Yes, Israel had sinned— and I am not minimizing this—but Joshua was also overconfident and did not seek the Lord before battle as he had before.

My point is that leading Israel was not just an assignment; it was a partnership, and Joshua left out the senior partner, God. You are a turnaround pastor, and you not only have an assignment but you also have a partnership with God.

And God not only believes you can do this job but He believes you are the best one to do this job. Otherwise, He would have sent someone else. God wants to be your number one fan and greatest cheerleader, but He also is your coach and mentor, instructor and teacher, leader and guide. He doesn't want to just turn you loose to get the job done; He wants to work with you to get the job done.

For example, when I was a boy, I loved building model airplanes. My dad bought me a complicated model of a P-51 Mustang. He'd hoped we could build it together, but I wanted to build it myself. I came to a point in its construction where I couldn't make some of the moving pieces work as they should, so I just glued them together.

It appeared to look fine, but the canopy didn't slide back or the wheels retract as they were originally capable of. I'd done it myself, but it didn't turn out quite right. My teacher later asked me if my dad had helped me.

I responded, "He wanted to, but I wanted to do it myself."

She smiled and said, "It looks good, Don, but I think you may have been happier with the results if you would have let your dad help you." I've never forgotten that lesson.

In leading our church's turnaround, I can honestly say I have become closer to Jesus than ever before. I hear His voice clearer, sense His encouragement more deeply, and see the broader purposes of His Kingdom better than ever before.

As a turnaround pastor, you have a unique and wonderful opportunity to experience the grace of God like few others. You get to work with Jesus to raise the dead. You get to see Him breathe life into others through you. Don't try and do this assignment alone. Recognize that Jesus has called you to "be strong and very courageous," but He has also called you to "ask counsel of the Lord" because being a turnaround pastor is a partnership. This leads me to my last piece of counsel.

THIS IS ABOUT JESUS AND YOU

As I reflect back on this season of leadership at our church and all the problems faced and lessons learned, one lesson rises above all others. It is summed up in words I first mentioned in chapter 6, and I'd like to take a minute and delve a little deeper.

Whatever problem you're facing is more about you and Jesus than you and the problem.

There is an amazing thought that as committed as Jesus is to building His church, He is just as committed to developing me as a leader. This means that He already knows and understands any problem I will face, and He already knows the answer.

I believe that Jesus wants us to learn that solving the problem is not the final goal. The goal is the relationship we have with Him. Whatever problem you are facing in your turnaround assignment, or whatever problem you are facing in your life, it is more about you and Jesus than you and the problem.

Let me explain. For years I lived as a transactional pastor with God as I sought to turn my church around. If I was faithful, read my Bible, behaved morally, paid my tithe, studied leadership, made the courageous decisions, and basically did all the right things, then I deserved success. In my mind, success meant a growing, vibrant church, which I knew Jesus wanted as well.

I was treating the challenge of solving a ministry problem like a transaction with God: if I do what I'm supposed to do, then God will do what He is supposed to do and give me success. Although this is true in a sense, it is a poor basis for a relationship. It means I am serving Him to get what I want, namely success. That is not serving; that is a transaction, and it is an attempt on my part to control God through my good works. That just isn't going to work.

When God revealed this part of my heart, it was a shock, and I was ashamed. When God asked me in prayer (chapter 6) if I would serve Him even our church never grew past 150, He was asking me if He was my reward or if a successful, growing church was my reward. My answer revealed whether I wanted Him or success more. His question penetrated my heart, and my deepest motives were quickly exposed. I could only repent.

The reason this is so important is that God has called turnaround pastors to call His people, and whoever will listen, into a relationship with Him. And since we all reproduce after our own kind, we will reproduce transactional disciples if we are transactional pastors.

If, however, we have learned that Jesus is the reward, our pearl of great price, then we will reproduce disciples who have a sweet relationship with God.

If I am transactional with God, then every setback and every painful experience means God did not come through. If I am transactional, then I will respond with, "God, I did my part, but you didn't do yours." Bitterness will creep in. Then I run the risk of not completing my turnaround assignment, perhaps quitting the ministry, and maybe even turning away from Jesus.

But if my relationship with Jesus is my portion and reward, then every problem brings a grateful heart. I am so grateful that I am not facing this situation alone. Then Jesus is leading me, and success becomes a gift from God, not to be a possession but something treasured and honored as a trust.

This is why every problem is more about Jesus and me, because how I respond to the problem reveals what's in my heart. When I give Jesus my heart, He in turn gives me His. When people see and feel Jesus' heart in me, they are drawn to the Jesus in me.

I am no longer trying to make a deal with God. I am in a place of peace and rest. I still work hard, but the results are honestly in His hands. Win or lose, we still win because we have the treasure in us.

Now success becomes His responsibility, not mine. As in Ezekiel, I only have to speak, and He breathes new life into the dry bones.

YOU CAN DO THIS

As a turnaround pastor, God has called you, and you can do this. Yes, it will take a sizeable portion of your life, but if Jesus has asked you to lead this turnaround, you seriously have nothing else to do. This is your assignment. So as Paul so eloquently says, do it with all your heart.

> *Whatever you do, work at it with all your heart, as working for the Lord, not for human masters, since you know that you will receive an inheritance from the Lord as a reward. It is the Lord Christ you are serving.*
> *Colossians 3:23–24*

There are thousands of pastors just like you, doing similar assignments. God is building an army of men and women who will not quit in their turnaround assignment. They will not turn back. They will persevere, and we will see amazing stories in the future of resurrected churches. My prayer is that you and your church will be one of those stories.

You can do this! A thousand years from now, when your time on earth is long gone, who will be in heaven with you because you said yes to becoming a turnaround pastor? More importantly, you can feel Jesus smiling right now, as you purpose in your heart to lead your church to accomplish the mission assigned to you.

TURNAROUNDCHURCH
COACHING NETWORK

I hope reading Turnaround Pastor has been a blessing to you. If you are interested in going to the next level in your leadership, then I suggest you consider joining the Turnaround Church Coaching Network. We'd be honored to have you be a part of this group as you seek to lead your church forward. Here are some frequently asked questions about TCCN.

What is TCCN? This is a nine-month coaching experience from September to May that includes reading two relevant books per month, group interaction, practical teaching and homework focused on building your church.

Where and when does TCCN meet? We will meet one Friday a month at Creekside Church from 9:00 am to 3:00 pm.

Why should I join TCCN? If your church is plateaued or is declining TCCN can help you get "unstuck" as a leader and help your church get moving again. While there are no guarantees, this coaching has been instrumental in helping many churches break through.

What are the coaching sessions like? The morning sessions focus on the heart and deal with the emotional and spiritual issues pastors face in leading a turnaround church. The afternoon sessions focus on the head, and deal with strategies and systems for leading an effective turnaround in your church.

How are TCCN Pastor's supported? While you are in the coaching network, several members of Creekside Church will be assigned to pray for you and communicate with you each month. You can share your most relevant prayer needs with them. In addition you will have email access to Don during the coaching year. You will also receive extensive practical ministry materials designed to help you move your church forward.

How can I get more info on TCCN regarding cost, application and current schedule? The best way to get more information is to visit our website at www.turnaroundchurch.org